D0734843

SEX KITTENS

SEX KITTENS
SINGLE CATS SEEKING SAME

CHRIS AKINS

Sterling Publishing
New York

A Sterling Book
Published by Sterling Publishing Co., Inc.
387 Park Avenue South, New York, NY 10016

Distributed in Canada by Sterling Publishing
c/o Canadian Manda Group, 165 Dufferin Street
Toronto, Ontario M6K 3H6

Distributed in Great Britain by Chrysalis Books
64 Brewery Road, London N79NT, England
Distributed in Australia by Capricorn Link (Australia) Pty. Ltd.
P.O. Box 704, Windsor, NSW 2756, Australia

While this book may seem to encourage animal mating, it is meant for entertainment pur-
poses only. Every day, tens of thousands of puppies and kittens are born, and every year
tens of thousands of dogs and cats cannot find a home and must be put to sleep as a
result. In order to help diminish the overpopulation, and consequent euthanasia, of stray
animals, please have your pet spayed or neutered. Thank you!

Library of Congress Cataloging-in-Publication Data

Akins, Chris.
   Sex kittens : single cats seeking same / Chris Akins.
         p. cm.
   Includes index.
   ISBN 1-4027-3447-6
 1. Cats—Humor. 2. Love—Humor. I. Title.

PN6231.C23A36 2005
818'.602—dc22

2005024366

Photography Editor: Chris Bain
Additional photo research: Janice Ackerman, Lori Epstein

Color separations by Friesens Corporation
Printed in Canada by Friesens Corporation

10 9 8 7 6 5 4 3 2 1

Table of Contents

Introduction

If you're reading this book, you're probably one of the millions of cats across the country who thinks that he or she is alone. But the truth is, you're not. That growling Siamese in the vet's waiting room? He's single. The Persian you occasionally see in the window across the street? Abstinent, through no fault of her own, since her adoption in 1992. The sad reality is nearly two in three cats today are living single, with no immediate prospects to remedy their solo plights.

You've probably already tried all of the basic routes, too, or you wouldn't be reading this right now. You've tried parties. Alleys. Random hook-ups in the park. Your sister's neighbor. Prowling at night like a common stray. Sometimes even your littermates, in a fit of desperation. But no matter how hard you keep looking, Mr. or Mrs. Right (or even a combination of the two) always seems to have passed through a day or so ahead of you, leaving behind only a scent of what could have been.

Mew no more! This book is here to help. It provides a way to discreetly check out the current state of the singles scene, and maybe even help you hook up with someone special. Maybe dogs are stupid enough to run up and lick the butts of every other canine they see, but cats are not so crude. As a cat, you not only have discriminating taste, but a sense of

propriety, a duty to maintain the social order, and above all a desire to be stylish and attractive. In *Sex Kittens*, you can browse the ads of other single cats in the privacy of your own home, and at your leisure.

The sections that follow are clearly divided into the most common groups to accommodate every taste. Pick the one that interests you and begin the hunt for your soul mate!

The Categories

Toms Seeking Queens

From teasers to bull toms, torties to tricksters, pedigreed show-toms to rough-around-the edges alley brawlers, there's a tom for every taste. Whether you're a discriminating queen or a gal on the prowl, you'll find that XY feline to satisfy your palate in "Toms Seeking Queens."

Queens Seeking Toms

Tired of taking a number behind every other tom in the neighborhood each time the kitty in 12B goes into heat? Check out the extensive selection in "Queens Seeking Toms," where you're sure to find that special lady who'll make you think of tongue-bathing in a whole new light.

Toms Seeking Toms

Daddys, twinks, bears, pubs (pedigreed urban breeds)—no matter your taste, there's a tom out there waiting for his tall-dark-and-handsome, and we've collected the best in our "Toms Seeking Toms" chapter. Will you be the one?

Queens Seeking Queens

Are you a queen looking for other queens and finding it hard to winnow out the chaff from the wheat? Our "Queens Seeking Queens" section offers a variety of eager queens, from lithe young tabbies to gals who've seen it all and then some.

Anything Goes

Maybe you're looking for an activity partner to join your neighborhood group. Perhaps your sensual appetites are a bit unorthodox. Or maybe you want a tom *and* a queen at the same time? While wearing a dog collar? Whatever your kink, you'll find something to satisfy it in the "Anything Goes" chapter.

The Code System

Knowing that you don't want to spend all your time deciphering long lists of codes and letters, this book keeps it as simple as possible.

P = **Purebred**
C = **Crossbred**

A = **Altered**
W = **Whole**

T = **Tom**
Q = **Queen**

For example, "PAT iso CWQ" means "Purebred Altered Tom in search of Crossbred Whole Queen." Don't worry, the code just provides a general guideline to help you narrow your search. Whether you end up finding a partner for life or a friend for the evening, well, we'll leave that up to you.

A Cat's Guide to Fishing and Hunting

Once you've browsed through *Sex Kittens* and found the perfect ad, it's time to meet your date. But perhaps you've been out of the dating scene for so long that you're afraid you'll ruin your big chance. Maybe you excel at stalking small prey, but freeze up when it comes to flirting with that cute tom down the block. And sometimes the haughty stare of a queen paralyzes you with fear.

Well, take a deep breath and relax—we're here to help.

As you have probably already realized, finding a potential partner is only the first step on the road to true love (or whatever it is you're in search of). Once you've found that kindred spirit, you'll naturally want to get to know him or her better. But hang on for just one second there, kitty cat! Before you rush headlong into the unknown, here are some important tips and guidelines that will make your first contact safe and successful. This is all for your own (physical and emotional) protection—the current dating scene is a jungle, and our experienced matchmakers have a lot of valuable advice to share that will help you navigate the tall grasses of the single cat's search for love.

Safety

- Avoid strange alleys
- Always tell your friends where you're going
- If it's a first date, meet for lunch in a public place
- Don't give out personal contact information until you get to know your date better
- Look for telltale signs of trouble in your date: missing ears or tail segments; missing teeth; an eye patch; constant, repetitive scratching
- If the tree looks taller than the ones in your yard, don't climb it
- Always smell for dog before jumping over any fence
- Keep your tail lowered if you don't trust your date (this goes for toms, too)
- Try not to go on a date right after having your claws trimmed; for first dates, especially, the blunt nubs will offer almost no sting should you need to set boundaries
- If you've been declawed, *never* meet a new date in a private location; it could be a trap
- Carry a tiny spray bottle of water with you, in case you need to dissuade your dinner date from following you home at the end of the evening

Grooming
- Check for litter between your claws before going out
- Remember, nobody likes a bushy tail. If you're feeling that on-edge, excuse yourself and try to reschedule the date (or cancel it entirely)
- Queens! No matter how much you like him, try not to sound or act like you're in heat—unless you *are* in heat, in which case we all know how the date's going to end up anyway
- If you've been meaning to clean the inside of that hind leg for a while, do it *before* you go out in public

Etiquette
- Don't crowd the food bowl
- If you've been invited to his or her place, bring a gift— half a cicada, for instance, or a newborn mouse (or for you city cats, a dirty take-out container)
- Toms! Don't immediately sniff her butt—try to say hello first and let her grow comfortable
- If you run into old flames while on your date, avoid hissing uncontrollably
- When using a new litter box, remember to *always cover completely*
- It's an unpleasant reality that many cats find the Siamese dialect off-putting. Rather than risk an uncomfortable encounter, try to find out discreetly beforehand

Follow these simple guidelines and you'll soon be purring happily with your new friend, lover, or bridge partner. And remember, at first it's just a date, not Judgment Day! Stay calm, be alert, always be yourself, and *have fun*. If humans can do it, it can't be that hard.

Happy Hunting!

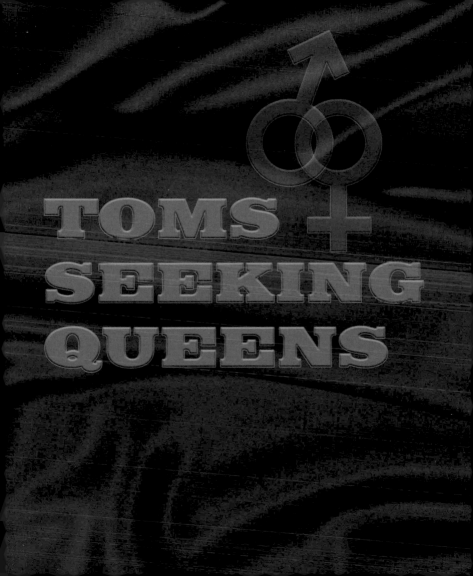

TOMS SEEKING QUEENS

Lion in Search of Pride

WHAT I'M LOOKING FOR: CWT wants a P/CW queen with a fire in her belly who knows who wears the claws in this family. No spays; I need a queen who can provide me with lots of little lions.

WHY YOU WANT TO GET TO KNOW ME: I'll take good care of you. I'll fight for you. I'm a take-charge kind of tom who won't hesitate to set the record straight. In fact, I love to fight! Gimme another tom, or, better yet, a human leg, and I'll show everyone who's the king of this house.

WHAT I'M LISTENING TO/WATCHING: On TV: Dr. Phil, all of those *When Animals Attack!* specials. Listening to: Lynyrd Skynyrd, Charlie Daniels.

MY FAVORITE PHYSICAL ACTIVITIES: Biting, hissing, scratching, clawing legs, improving my ear-flattening response time, looking for things to back up under while hissing and/or growling, and chasing bees.

A SECRET MOST OTHERS DON'T KNOW ABOUT ME: Although whole, I only have one testicle. But I was born that way, so don't make fun of it or I'll pop ya.

MY MOTTO: It can't hurt you if you hurt it first.

SEX KITTENS 16

EASY TO LOVE

WHAT I'M LOOKING FOR: CAT wants CAQ who enjoys the same things I enjoy, like lying around all day and eating.

WHY YOU WANT TO GET TO KNOW ME: I'm easygoing and good tempered. You'll never find me out tomcatting around, or picking unnecessary fights. I like furniture and lots of it.

MY IDEAL DATE INCLUDES: My owner leaves the cabinet door open wide enough to tear into the cat food, and we eat as much as we want, then retire to the bedroom for a hardcore food coma.

MY FAVORITE PHYSICAL ACTIVITIES: You gotta be kidding me. There are parts of my body I haven't licked in years.

WHAT'S IN MY BEDROOM: A cat bed for afternoon naps, a fur-lined blanket for short catch-up naps, and an old box with a cat toy in the corner, for quick morning naps.

MY MOTTO: You know what they say: big belly, big napping pillow!

SEX
KITTENS
17

I Don't Sleep, I Pass Out

WHAT I'M LOOKING FOR: Groupies! CAT seeks P/C A/W queens—any hot chicks who just wanna have fun and stay up all night. If you aren't still awake when the sun rises, you're doing something wrong.

WHY YOU WANT TO GET TO KNOW ME: 'Cause I'm a rock star, baby! I figure you only live nine times, right? Why waste it on keeping your nose clean and doing what you're told? Life's too short! I go where the night takes me.

WHAT I'M LISTENING TO: Death From Above 1979, Bloc Party, The Cramps, Peaches, Gaza Strippers.

WHAT'S IN MY BEDROOM: The world is my bedroom, baby! But seriously, my room's a mess: empty cough syrup bottles, a cigarette butt, part of a mouse, the rank odor of whiskey sweat, hairballs, a couple of strange cats I think I met the night before but whose names I've forgotten, and at least one pile of cat vomit.

A SECRET MOST OTHERS DON'T KNOW ABOUT ME: I'm afraid of vacuum cleaners.

SEX KITTENS 18

MY MOTTO: No queen's too ugly if you're drunk enough.

Alternative Lifestylist Needs Counterbalance

From: tom651
Sent: Sunday, June 22, 2005 @ 4:21 PM
To: PAQ
Subject: RE: Alternative Lifestylist Needs Counterbalance

WHAT I'M LOOKING FOR: PAT looking for a PAQ with a background different than mine, someone who's grounded and full of the common sense I lack, but who isn't a wet blanket.

WHY YOU WANT TO GET TO KNOW ME: I'm a crazy tom who leaps before he looks. Sometimes I find myself in messy situations, but life's no fun if you don't take risks! I love movies, midnight strolls through strange backyards, and scrounging for alternative sources of food and water. Maybe I don't always have perfect manners, but who cares? Manners are for lap dogs.

WHAT'S IN MY BEDROOM: An empty cat food tin I found in someone else's garbage, a couple of bird parts, some string, 300 yards of unraveled toilet paper, and a bunch of toenail clippings.

MY IDEAL DATE INCLUDES: An ideal date would be one where we could both show each other a different experience. I would take you on a midnight prowl of the neighborhood garbage cans, and then you would accompany me home and show me what it means to be truly clean.

MY MOTTO: Heaven is a stinky dumpster.

SEX KITTENS 19

Keeping Cool Until I Find the Right One

WHAT I'M LOOKING FOR: PWT seeks fun and adventure with a happy-go-lucky P/C A/W queen. Maybe you're that special someone to settle down with for the long haul, but even if you're not, we can still figure out how to use the microwave together.

WHY YOU WANT TO GET TO KNOW ME: I'm a funny and hyper tom with a good sense of humor. Plus I know how to get into the fridge.

BEST/WORST/BIGGEST LIE I EVER TOLD: When I was adopted, my owners actually wanted to adopt my brother—so when they weren't looking, I pushed him under our siblings and started posing like him. My owners didn't notice the difference and adopted me instead. Ha ha! Sorry about that, Claude.

MY FAVORITE PHYSICAL ACTIVITIES: Turning things on and off when I'm the only one home, figuring out how doors work, and planning the doom of all things that fly.

MY MOTTO: Who put the milk container back in the fridge with this tiny little bit left? Who!?

Purr-fect!

SEX KITTENS 20

High-Strung Bachelor Needs Soothing Touch

What I'm Looking For: PWT seeks PWQ, specifically Siamese, with an excellent pedigree, to carry on my highly respectable, if somewhat twitchy, bloodline.

Why You Want To Get To Know Me: I have impeccable taste. I like to keep things very clean, whether it's my super-glossy coat or my neatly raked and gridded litter box. I enjoy the company of top-of-the-line felines and furniture (see photo of my new cat bed, a mid-twentieth-century Burgess & Leigh Burleigh Ware cat coddle).

My Dream Vacation: I dream of a comfortable chateau somewhere in the north of France, where the mousing is superb and the children sparse and afraid of being slashed.

Best/Worst/Biggest Lie I Ever Told: I told a tabby down the block that I was fixed, then never talked to her again.

I'm Most Neurotic About: Having any crossbred offspring show up to claim I'm their father, not having a narrow-enough head for my pedigree, going bald.

My Motto: Some cats are more equal than others.

SEX KITTENS 21

I Have So Much Love to Give

WHAT I'M LOOKING FOR: I'm a generously proportioned CAT who needs an activity partner and a friend, but most of all, a soul mate. Nobody wants to be alone. If you're a solo P/CAQ who's still looking for Tom Right, how about giving Tom "White" a try?

WHY YOU WANT TO GET TO KNOW ME: I have a lot of love to offer, first of all, but there's more. I also love to laugh, and I love to give and receive attention. You will always find me eager to play, day or night—I'm not one of those toms who says he's too sleepy for a little impromptu scuffle. I love to sit in the window and watch the great outdoors (I'll watch whatever's "on," but my favorites include birds, dogs, and ants).

WHAT I'M READING/LISTENING TO/WATCHING: Reading: Jonathan Livingston Seagull (for about the sixteenth time!). On TV: Extreme Makeover Home Edition (even though it always makes me cry, lol!) Listening to: Celine Dion's greatest hits.

MY IDEAL DATE INCLUDES: Anything, so long as it involves a good time being spent with that special queen. Could it be you?

A SECRET MOST OTHERS DON'T KNOW ABOUT ME: My last girlfriend ran away without any warning over a year ago. I still can't figure out why. Don't worry, "my heart will go on!" ;-)

MY MOTTO: A hug is a custom-fit rainbow!

SEX
KITTENS
22

PERSONALS

NO MORE GAMES

WHAT I'M LOOKING FOR: PWT wants PA/WQ who's honest, loyal, and open. Someone who respects me for me. A queen I can trust. No diabetics, please.

WHY YOU WANT TO GET TO KNOW ME: I'm down-to-earth, loyal, and I get things done. If I say I love you, then I love you. I don't lie and I hate liars. If you want kittens, fine, I can take 'em or leave 'em, just tell me up front. Don't play games with me and we'll get along great.

WHAT'S IN MY BEDROOM: The same cat bed I've had since I was a kitten. A plastic ball that I keep neatly positioned in the same spot every day. A plastic dish with two evenly sized areas—one side contains food and the other side contains water. A medium-size litter box in the corner, which I keep meticulously neat.

MY IDEAL DATE INCLUDES: For the first hour or so we would keep to ourselves on opposite sides of the room, while I sized you up. Finally, when I began to sense you relax, I would ignore you and go eat. Afterwards, you would come up and eat. Then we would fall asleep near each other. Frenzied love-making to follow.

I'M MOST NEUROTIC ABOUT: Disorder, having a dirty butt, matted hair, and having my whiskers touched.

MY MOTTO: God is in the details.

SEX KITTENS 23

Birds of a Feather (Taste Good Together)

WHAT I'M LOOKING FOR: A CAQ who's not too domesticated, for long, lazy afternoons in the backyard and nearby woods. Must be independent and unafraid of nature. Must have own claws. Good hunters preferred.

WHY YOU WANT TO GET TO KNOW ME: I'm a nature-lover at heart. Into bird watching, bird eating. Can survive for several weeks outdoors, and have a great sense of direction and smell. I'm adventurous, friendly, and relaxed. If you're easy going, you're sure to have a good time with me.

WHAT I'M WATCHING: My favorite movie is *The Birds*— I drool through pretty much the whole thing, but that last scene is heaven. How did Hitch do that to all those birds?

MY FAVORITE PHYSICAL ACTIVITIES: Hunting. Runner up: spending the afternoon on a sun-dappled lawn, preferably a slightly overgrown one, waiting for the perfect moment to strike.

SEX KITTENS 24

MY MOTTO: If you build it, they will come, and then you can eat them.

Can't a Nice Cat Finish First?

WHAT I'M LOOKING FOR: CAT iso healthy and sane P/CA queen who can recognize a good catch when she sees one, who doesn't think brains are everything, and who looks forward to long baths and warm naps with her special guy.

WHY YOU WANT TO GET TO KNOW ME: I'm a simple cat, but I'm honest and loyal. I don't mind sharing, whether it's food, a bed, or attention from my masters. Sometimes I like to go out mousing with the neighborhood toms, but I'm always back by morning.

MY IDEAL DATE INCLUDES: We would eat some special "Holiday Food"—canned instead of dry—then go on a tour of my property. If we hit it off, I'd love to show you my secret space on the roof of the house, where I go to nap on sunny afternoons.

A SECRET MOST OTHERS DON'T KNOW ABOUT ME: I'm not a good judge of distance when I jump.

MY MOTTO: Keep it simple and you'll live longer.

SEX KITTENS 25

Need to Get Out More

WHAT I'M LOOKING FOR: PWT seeks free-spirited crossbred queen who is unpretentious and incapable of getting pregnant to bring this lonely, latchkey bachelor out of his shell.

WHY YOU WANT TO GET TO KNOW ME: I'm a healthy, in-shape guy who's tired of being cooped up by cost-sensitive owners who couldn't afford me in the first place. Looking to step out, if you know what I mean, for a night of high-kicking caterwauling, no strings attached. Funny, athletic, will try anything at least a couple of times.

MY DREAM VACATION: Going camping out in the middle of nowhere, and being a free-range cat for a week.

MY FAVORITE PHYSICAL ACTIVITIES: Jumping out of hidey-holes to surprise-attack the humans, taunting the dog by slapping him when he's asleep, pushing breakable objects off of high places, and trying to escape.

MY MOTTO: Let my people go!

SEX KITTENS
26

Retired and Ready for Love

What I'm Looking For:
CAT wants P/CAQ for dinner companion, maybe more. Must have a sense of humor, not be stuck-up or too finicky. Doesn't nag! Has a healthy "live and let live" attitude. Enjoys just sitting and staring for long stretches of time. Would be joining a household that's about to be an "empty nest," so must be able to put up with unnatural amounts of attention from humans for a while.

Why You Want To Get To Know Me: I'm a mind-my-own-business kind of tom, and don't get too worked up over anything. I've seen it all, and you'll never catch me telling you what I think you should do. I'm a creature of habit and I don't like having my routine interrupted, so if you like predictable, look no further.

My Ideal Date Includes: I'm a real homebody, so I'd prefer to stay in for the evening. We could nap at sunset by the western windows in the master bedroom, then have a quiet dinner and curl up on the back of the couch.

I'm Most Neurotic About: Sudden, loud noises, fast-moving feet, and any group of humans greater than two.

My Motto: After my retirement party (see photo), I vowed, never again!

SEX KITTENS 27

Taste My Love Snacks

From: tom365
Sent: Wednesday, May 11, 2005 @ 4:57 PM
To: CAQ
Subject: RE: Taste My Love Snacks

WHAT I'M LOOKING FOR: CAT wants CAQ with an appetite for romance, love, and frozen food. I've got the run of the house most every day, and I need a lady with a curious temperament and a deep appreciation for culinary adventures. Must be able to help open doors, drawers, cabinets, and cardboard/plastic packages. Can-opener skills would be a big plus.

WHY YOU WANT TO GET TO KNOW ME: I haven't gone a day on just cat food since I was about 4 months old—and with me, neither will you.

WHAT I'M WATCHING: Ocean's 11, To Catch a Thief. Don't like TV, but I do enjoy staring at the aquarium and trying to figure out how to get in there without getting wet.

WHAT'S IN MY BEDROOM: The lid to an old pudding cup, a butter wrapper, some sugar packets, a dirty Popsicle stick, and some dried-up chunk of food that I haven't identified yet. (Smoked eel? Cow cheeks? Anyway, I'm working on it.)

MY MOTTO: Curiosity is an aphrodisiac—can you feel it?

SEX KITTENS 28

ALL YOU NEED IS LOVE

WHAT I'M LOOKING FOR: A fun-loving, sophisticated PWQ with a good ear who can appreciate kick-ass music, whether it's from Liverpool or Memphis. I don't want a music snob, but someone who knows the good stuff from the white noise and can

appreciate a record collection equal in value to an average-sized student loan.

WHY YOU WANT TO GET TO KNOW ME: I'll treat my lady like an original reel-to-reel studio recording of "Strawberry Fields Forever"—I'll keep you safe from the greasy paws of poseurs who couldn't possibly appreciate your uniqueness and exceptional value.

MY DREAM VACATION: I can think of several: a midnight prowl around the Chelsea Hotel in NYC, a nap in the studio of Sun Records in Nashville, or an afternoon stroll through the streets of Liverpool.

I'M MOST NEUROTIC ABOUT: Anything happening to my record collection. Humidity.

A SECRET MOST OTHERS DON'T KNOW ABOUT ME: I own Crystal Gayle's first album, and I still listen to it on days when I'm feeling blue.

MY MOTTO: Lovemaking should always be in stereo.

SEX KITTENS 29

Meow!

Better Safe Than Sorry

WHAT I'M LOOKING FOR:
I'm a CWT, wanting a PWQ.
You: be a self-sufficient, fertile
queen committed to helping
me start a new society far
away from corrupt, godless
humans.

**WHY YOU WANT TO GET
TO KNOW ME:** I have extensive field training in survival in
both natural and urban wilder-
nesses. Can hunt and catch
any game. Have all my claws.
I know better than to trust
humans.

**WHAT I'M
READING/WATCHING:**
I love watching old Charlton
Heston movies, especially *Ben
Hur* and *The Omega Man*; I've practically memorized the immortal *How to
Survive in the Woods*.

BEST/WORST/BIGGEST LIE I EVER TOLD: Every time a human pets
me or rubs my ears, I purr as if I actually enjoy it.

I'M MOST NEUROTIC ABOUT: The steady, cumulative erosion of
feline rights. I think I was implanted with a tracking device "for my
safety" the last time I was at the vet!

MY MOTTO: They can take my claws from my cold, dead paws.

SEX
KITTENS
30

Hungry for Love

WHAT I'M LOOKING FOR: PAT iso an old-fashioned CAQ who likes to make her special tom feel like a king. I'll protect and love you; you'll turn my bachelor pad into a happy home. You know the secret to a tom's heart is through his stomach. Prefer shorthairs. Must like pepperoni.

WHY YOU WANT TO GET TO KNOW ME: I'm a good listener. Plus, I'm passionate about three things: food, sleep, and licking my partner's ears clean several times a day.

MY IDEAL DATE INCLUDES: You'd make me a big, hearty, old-world-style meal, wearing nothing but your silky short fur and a smile, while I sniff your butt and rub my head against your thighs. Me-OW!

I'M MOST NEUROTIC ABOUT: My humans dying outside the home, and then nobody coming around to clean my litter box or tip the pizza-delivery guy.

MY MOTTO: Love is a dish best made in the kitchen.

SEX
KITTENS
31

Let Me Show You My World

WHAT I'M LOOKING FOR: PWT iso self-confident PAQ who isn't too clingy, can keep her distance when necessary, and who is eager to discover the refreshing and bountiful world of toilet water.

WHY YOU WANT TO GET TO KNOW ME: I have unrestricted access to a premium, unfiltered pool of water that's self-replenishing, (almost) always crystal clear, and untouched by human hands. Imagine: A private bath, a fountain of intoxicating liquid always at the ready! Not many creatures in this world live a life of such luxury. Come taste the experience with me.

I'M MOST NEUROTIC ABOUT: Finding the lid down; floaters.

MY FAVORITE PHYSICAL ACTIVITIES: Splashing, making wet paw-print patterns all over the house.

MY MOTTO: "Take me to the river, drop me in the water" (figuratively speaking, of course).

Hottie!

SEX KITTENS 32

Black Panther

What I'm Looking For: Mad-as-hell CWT searching for a self-actualized CQ, whole or altered, who's proud of her heritage and committed to the fight for greater rights for cats all over the world.

Why You Want To Get To Know Me: I'm a strong believer in catkind's rights, and I'm a fighter. I believe nothing is more powerful than the desires of the feline heart, and once I set my mind on something, I never give up on it.

What I'm Reading/Watching: *Free the Animals: The Story of the Animal Liberation Front,* by Ingrid Newkirk, *Animal Liberation,* by Peter Singer. No TV—the Animal Planet channel makes me sick to my stomach and anyway, the revolution will not be televised.

A Secret Most Others Don't Know About Me: Sometimes at night I stare at the sleeping, bourgeois lumps in the bed and imagine quietly slitting their throats, ushering in an age where cats rule the earth.

My Motto: Fight the power! Zoo=prison.

SEX KITTENS
33

Feel the Rush!

From: tom394
Sent: Sunday, June 12, 2005 @ 1:40 PM
To: CA/WQ
Subject: RE: Feel the Rush!

WHAT I'M LOOKING FOR: Thrill-seeking CAT wants adventurous, risk-taking CA/WQ who likes to live life a little closer to the edge than most felines. Armchair kitties need not apply.

WHY YOU WANT TO GET TO KNOW ME: I'll show you a good time! There's never a dull moment around me. I love to seek out new places—there's no shelf or branch too high. I'm very competitive, but I would throw the whole X Games career aside for the right pussycat.

WHAT I'M READING/WATCHING: My favorite book is *DogTown: The Legend of the Z-Boys*. I don't watch much TV, but I play a lot of *Tony Hawk's Underground* on my PlayStation 2.

MY IDEAL DATE INCLUDES: We break into the local aquarium (top floor, loose window pane) and make our way down past the laser-alarm system to the rare tropical fish hall. Laughing into our collars and slurping precious show fish along the way, we head back to the roof. We leap the three stories to the ground, coupling in mid-air.

MY MOTTO: Catch air, get vert, go for it!

SEX KITTENS

34

PERSONAL

OWNER OF A BROKEN HEART

WHAT I'M LOOKING FOR: Lovelorn, desperate CAT seeks Florence Nightingale with attraction to lost causes. You are a CAQ with a gentle touch and the cure for a broken heart. No neatniks, please.

WHY YOU WANT TO GET TO KNOW ME: I'm a smart, sensitive tom, but I've just ended a long-term relationship and my feelings are a little raw. She broke up with me on Christmas Eve, and as you can see from my photo, Santa's best efforts did nothing to improve my condition. Bring me back to life and we'll contemplate its mysteries together: Why does the dry food in the kitchen? What is it with plastic shopping bags? And should I go outside, or not?

WHAT'S IN MY BEDROOM: A dozen photographs of happier times, with a certain heartless feline's face cut out of every one; every letter she ever wrote me; and ticket stubs from the Broadway production of *I Love You, You're Perfect, Now Change* from that magical trip we took to New York City.

MOTTO: Oh, what tangled balls of yarn we weave when we strive to deceive.

SEX KITTENS 35

My Love Is Not of This World

WHAT I'M LOOKING FOR: Brilliant, reclusive CAT seeks C/PAQ with brains—you'll be the Scully to my Mulder. You know, like I do, that we're not being told the whole story, and you'll stop at nothing to get to the bottom of the conspiracy. Orange fur preferred.

WHY YOU WANT TO GET TO KNOW ME: I'm smart and self-sufficient, and ever since I was abducted by aliens, I can read the human "language" and I have X-ray vision. I have a secret stash of food and supplies in case we ever need to disappear for a little while. My litter box is lined with foil (good against both leakage and alien mind probes).

WHAT I'M WATCHING: On TV: *Veronica Mars, The Dead Zone*. On DVD: *Brazil*, all nine seasons of *The X-Files*.

A SECRET MOST OTHERS DON'T KNOW ABOUT ME: I hear voices from the Other Side, and it creeps me out—sometimes it looks like I'm jumping into the air for no reason, but it's because of Them!

I'M MOST NEUROTIC ABOUT: Implants in my teeth, the vet (definitely an alien), any sort of flashing light, and the possibility that the birds around my house might be bionic.

MY MOTTO: The truth really isn't out there, in the open. It's actually hidden inside a big government warehouse somewhere.

SEX KITTENS
36

From: tom623579
Sent: Tuesday, April 26, 2005 @ 11:05 AM
To: P/CAQ
Subject: Angel in the Daylight, Devil Under the Sheets

WHAT I'M LOOKING FOR: PAT seeks hot P/CAQs with tight bodies and great flexibility. Yowlers a plus. Be unashamed of your body and eager to have a good time.

WHY YOU WANT TO GET TO KNOW ME: I'm confident, enthusiastic, and a great lover (no, really). I take care of a female's needs, and I will treat you like a real queen.

WHAT I'M READING/LISTENING TO/WATCHING: On TV: *Blind Date*. Reading: *The Sexual Life of Catherine M.*, by Catherine Millet. Listening to: Sade, Luther Vandross.

WHAT'S IN MY BEDROOM: Some candles, a luxurious bed, cushions, toys in all shapes and sizes, a little chest of catnip on a small, low coffee table, and a heady, musky scent in the air.

MY IDEAL DATE INCLUDES: We would make sweet, loud love all night, pausing only to replenish our bodies with food and drink, and when we could no longer go on, we'd collapse blissfully into sleep.

MY MOTTO: "You. And me. And her. Simultaneous— You. And me. And you, and you! Simultaneous lovin', baby. Two or three, heh heh...."

SEX
KITTENS
37

Living Large, Loving Lean

WHAT I'M LOOKING FOR: Self-made CAT wants beautiful, well-groomed PAQ who doesn't need to talk 24/7 and who enjoys taking care of her tom.

WHY YOU WANT TO GET TO KNOW ME: I'm handsome, I live in a good home, and I smell great! If you're the kind of queen who dreams of curling up in the lap of luxury, and who wants to do your curling with a tom of means, then we should arrange to meet. (No gold-diggers, please!)

WHAT'S IN MY BEDROOM: The latest issue of *Cat Fancy*, a collection of cologne samples from my human's magazines (I'm a collector), an empty shampoo bottle I use as a toy, a cat comb, and a fluffy eiderdown bed. (I keep my litter box far away in the basement, where it belongs.)

MY DREAM VACATION: A weekend getaway with that special pussy (you?) at an all-inclusive spa and resort, where we would be pampered and massaged, have our claws trimmed, and be treated like the royal felines we are.

A SECRET MOST OTHERS DON'T KNOW ABOUT ME: I was homeless for about a year when I was younger.

MY MOTTO:
Living well
is the best
revenge!

SEX
KITTENS
38

Did You Hear the One About the Three Blind Mice?

What I'm Looking For: PWT seeks PAQ with great sense of humor who loves to laugh, play, and generally have a good time. Fun times and companionship only—I'm not ready to settle down.

Why You Want To Get To Know Me: Because you're guaranteed to have fun. Even if my jokes don't always land, I've got more of them than a mouse has blood vessels. And I love to play tricks on my human companions—it's hilarious to watch them fight over who left the TV on or search for their "misplaced" socks.

What's In My Bedroom: What it looks like to my humans: an old cat bed, a couple of toys, a collar that they can't seem to keep on me. What it's really like: Treasure Island! I've got over a dozen small valuables hidden in my bed and the surrounding area, mostly things that the humans have "lost" over the years.

Best/Worst/Biggest Lie I Ever Told: I once broke a glass by pushing it off the counter, but escaped undetected. I came around the corner yawning and blinking my eyes sleepily, then stared in bewilderment at the mess. The humans totally bought it!

My Motto: Who's ever going to believe that the cat put the car keys into the Insinkerator!?

From: tom22
Sent: Monday, May 16, 2005 @ 5:30 AM
To: CAQ
Subject: RE: Barely Keeping It Together

WHAT I'M LOOKING FOR: A kind, smart CAQ who can bring me back from the edge. I need a lot of TLC from a cat who is patient and can nurse me back to emotional health.

WHY YOU WANT TO GET TO KNOW ME: I'm very loving and loyal—my ex would say "suffocating," but is it a crime to love too much? Anyway, I have yet to leave the house since the breakup and subsequent restraining order, but if there's another queen out there who can handle real affection (and lots of it), I'm willing to give it a shot.

WHAT I'M READING/LISTENING TO: Reading: *Queens in Heat*—a book of erotica (yeah, I admit it), *Toms Are from Mars, Queens Are from Venus*; Listening to: *69 Love Songs*, by the Magnetic Fields.

A SECRET MOST OTHERS DON'T KNOW ABOUT ME: My mother left my father for his sister.

I'M MOST NEUROTIC ABOUT: Opening up my heart to someone and having them crush it like an empty can of Fancy Feast.

MY MOTTO: If at first you don't succeed, try one more time (but that's it).

SEX KITTENS
40

PERSONAL

I'M GONNA EAT YOU UP BABY

WHAT I'M LOOKING FOR: Long-haired CAT iso tasty PAQ for a little home cookin', wildcat style. You bring that tasty rump roast, I'll bring the love sauce.

WHY YOU WANT TO GET TO KNOW ME: I'm a husky tom with an insatiable appetite—for food, play, and, most of all, extra helpings of sweet, sweet loving. Here, baby, let me clean those whiskers for you with my egg-beater.

WHAT'S IN MY BEDROOM: A big bottle of chocolate sauce, a box of foil, some butter, whipped cream, dried cranberries, and a very messy bed.

I'M MOST NEUROTIC ABOUT: Having my owners suddenly turn vegetarian—and then deciding that it should apply to the entire family diet, including mine.

MY FAVORITE PHYSICAL ACTIVITIES: Licking my chops, licking your chops.

MY MOTTO: Everything's better with gravy.

Hunky Stud!

SEX KITTENS 41

Regular Jack Looking for Regular Jill

WHAT I'M LOOKING FOR: CAT wants CAQ who's into the creature comforts of home: TV, salty snacks, and plenty of beer. My idea of a good time involves ESPN and a long, lazy day on the couch. Marriage-obsessed queens who are constantly on the prowl, dedicated mousers, and planners need not apply.

WHY YOU WANT TO GET TO KNOW ME: If the description above didn't turn you off, then we just might be spiritual littermates. I'm easy-going and laaaazy, and I'm not ashamed to say so.

WHAT'S IN MY BEDROOM: A couch, a recliner, a coffee table, a large TV, and way too much foot traffic. But to be honest, as far as I'm concerned, every room is my bedroom and people and animals alike do way too much walking around.

MY DREAM VACATION: A week locked in a mattress store—a mattress store with a TV department, beer dispenser, and popcorn maker!

I'M MOST NEUROTIC ABOUT: Being chased by a dog or a child—really, about having to exert myself at all.

MY MOTTO: Everything in life should come with a remote control.

SEX KITTENS 42

Irish Lumberjack with Plenty of Wood

From: tom1001
Sent: Friday, May 27, 2005 @ 1:25 AM
To: P/CAQ
Subject: RE: Irish Lumberjack with Plenty of Wood

WHAT I'M LOOKING FOR: CWT seeks P/CAQ—a spry young lass who's into snuggling under the flannel for long naps, and who loves to play "clean the body pillow" for hours at a time. I love to cuddle, and am iso a sleepy, warm queen to be my girlfriend.

WHY YOU WANT TO GET TO KNOW ME: I'm an independently wealthy young bachelor with wisdom of the ages. I'm easygoing usually, though I do have a fiery temper when provoked—usually when it comes to dealing with humans.

WHAT'S IN MY BEDROOM: There's a cat bed for me somewhere, but my real bedroom is the master bedroom, where there's a king-size sleep oasis that I call my own whenever it's not occupied by a human. (And when it is occupied, I gently pry my humans' eyelids open with my index claw until they get the hell out of it.)

MY IDEAL DATE INCLUDES: After a big pre-hibernation meal, we would climb under the covers of the bed and work our way down to the foot. We'd clean each other for a few minutes, briefly hump, then hunker down for a good three-hour nap.

A SECRET MOST OTHERS DON'T KNOW ABOUT ME:
I can't see very well in the dark.

MY MOTTO: Making love is better when it's between the sheets.

SEX
KITTENS
43

Dairy Junkie

WHAT I'M LOOKING FOR: Attractive, kind-hearted PAQ who is willing to go to Dairy Eaters Anonymous (DEA) meetings with me and to put a lock on the freezer when the milk-fat demon possesses me. I just need a little firm discipline to help me stop binging on sweet, sweet cream.

WHY YOU WANT TO GET TO KNOW ME: I'm a PAT with an insatiable hunger—for butter as well as for life. I am intensely loyal, intelligent, and I make a mean crème brulée.

WHAT'S IN MY BEDROOM: Old Good Humor wrappers, an empty jumbo tub of Edy's Vanilla Fudge Pie ice cream, and emergency packets of non-dairy creamer that I have been known to snort in desperate times.

MY DREAM VACATION: I would love to be taken to the Ben & Jerry's ice cream factory in Vermont, strapped into a harness, and lowered by crane into a ten-ton vat of Chubby Hubby.

I'M MOST NEUROTIC ABOUT: My weight.

MY MOTTO: I admit it: I ate the Frusen Gladje—and I'd do it again, too, if Häagen Dazs hadn't sued them into the ground.

SEX
KITTENS
44

Spit-Clean This Dirty Boy

What I'm Looking For: A lady friend—purebred, crossbred, altered, whole, I love 'em all—who'll help me reach those hidden spots, both on my coat and in my heart.

Why You Want To Get To Know Me: It took years of yogic training to be able to contort my body in ways that are unimaginable for mere mortal cats—let's not let that go to waste! And, anyone who can touch their tongue to their nose is worth knowing, don't you think?

What's In My Bedroom: I have a tiger-striped cat tent where I like to keep my string collection—it doubles as my tantric love nest. I also have a small vibrator, for that extra frisson....

My Ideal Date Includes: You'd come over at night, having already eaten and bathed. I flip the multicolored spotlights on in my tent, you shave and put on your pasties, and start the show. Finally, you'd give me a lap dance and offer to take me to the edge of desire!

My Motto: The feline form is a beautiful thing.

SEX KITTENS
45

Nudist Ready to Bare His Soul

WHAT I'M LOOKING FOR: PAT looking for shameless P/CA/WQ to experience life au naturel with a free-spirited naturist. You: long-limbed, red-haired, and fancy free. Sorry—if you're a Taurus, you'll have to take your bull elsewhere.

WHY YOU WANT TO GET TO KNOW ME: I'm peace-loving, gentle, intelligent, and I love myself (in a good way). I can have a conversation about the finer points of traveling cross-country in the company of human children one minute and the details of cat-door repair the next.

MY DREAM VACATION: I love to go camping, especially along a lake or river where I can spend the day stretched out on my back, soaking up the sun, my package dangling out there for the whole world to see.

A SECRET MOST OTHERS DON'T KNOW ABOUT ME: I'm balding a little on my ears, but I comb over them so it's hard to tell.

MY MOTTO: If you've got it, flaunt it!

SEX KITTENS 46

PERSONALS
DESPERATE HOUSEPETS DATING SERVICE

WRITE RIGHT NOW

WHAT I'M LOOKING FOR: PWT needs smart, educated CW queen to help finish the real-life adventure he's living. I'm the dashing swain, you're the femme fatale. Be beautiful inside and out, and always look sexy (especially when in danger).

WHY YOU WANT TO GET TO KNOW ME: I have a rich inner life and I'm very creative. I'm protective of my queens and pamper them silly. I also have an excellent costume collection and love going to masked balls.

WHAT I'M READING: My favorite book is *The Three Musketeers* by Alexander Dumas.

MY IDEAL DATE INCLUDES: Dinner at a romantic treetop bird's nest filled with just-born peepers, followed by a rooftop tour of the neighborhood and a tryst under the moonlight—is that you by my side, defying the heavens to stop our love?

MY FAVORITE PHYSICAL ACTIVITIES: Daydreaming, procrastinating, drinking a lot of coffee, writing in frenzied bursts, drunken orgies, sleeping off hangovers, daydreaming, etc.

MY MOTTO: Drama, action, romance—I'm a triple threat!

Call Tonight!

SEX KITTENS 47

There Is No Try, Only Do

WHAT I'M LOOKING FOR: Young CAT movie fanatic wants P/C A/W queen—pretty much anything goes, so long as you're not vain or sniffy—to hang out with. Must like video games, movies, and late-night arguments over short-lived TV series.

WHY YOU WANT TO GET TO KNOW ME: I'm smart, playful, and a kitten at heart. Actually, I'm just a kitten, period, but I'm very precocious!

WHAT I'M WATCHING: DIVX bootlegs of the entire *Star Wars* sexology, *The Venture Brothers*, and *Dragonball Z*, and the controversial *SpongeBob XXX* that Nickelodeon wouldn't air (too much graphic sex and violence).

WHAT'S IN MY BEDROOM: The complete collection of the first issue of *Star Wars* toys, all in mint condition (except for Hammerhead, who had an unfortunate accident involving my tail, a glass of soda, and a pack of matches). I also have some great *Shrek* figurines and a *Dick Tracy* decoder ring that I rescued from a cereal box.

A SECRET MOST OTHERS DON'T KNOW ABOUT ME IS: I have mutant ninja powers!

MY MOTTO: "War not make one great—big bowl of vitamin-fortified, sweetened breakfast cereal make one great."

SEX KITTENS 48

Just Moved

WHAT I'M LOOKING FOR: CAT, new to the neighborhood, needs outgoing CAQ to show him around and provide an insider's view. No homebodies and no alcoholics, please! Must be open to long-term commitment and long-distance travel.

WHY YOU WANT TO GET TO KNOW ME: I'm warm-hearted and generous and I appreciate the diversity the world has to offer. If you're interested, one rainy night I will regale you with tales from my travels –I've lived in Alaska, India, Tanzania, the Czech Republic, Zambia, and New Zealand, and moused my way through many ports of call in between.

WHAT'S IN MY BEDROOM: Lots of boxes, piles of half-wadded newspaper, bubble wrap. Pictures of the Eiffel Tower, Victoria Falls, and the Sydney Opera House. My snow globe collection. Also, a necklace of shrunken mouse heads I picked up in Africa.

A SECRET MOST OTHERS DON'T KNOW ABOUT ME: I'm afraid of flying and need several Valium to survive long airplane rides without freaking out.

I'M MOST NEUROTIC ABOUT: Losing my passport.

MY MOTTO: "No matter where in the universe you go, there you are."

A House Is Not a Home

WHAT I'M LOOKING FOR: A mature CAQ to replace someone very special to me who recently departed. You: be good-hearted and sensitive to others' grief. Widows who have gone/are going through something similar (that's me at the wake in the photo) are especially welcome.

WHY YOU WANT TO GET TO KNOW ME: I'm an old-fashioned tom, now retired, who likes to keep himself busy on weekdays patrolling for mice. I like to take it easy on the weekends, especially in the company of a special lady (you?). I've been told I can be moody, but all I ask for is a little peace and quiet in the afternoons when I nap, and I'm a happy camper.

A SECRET MOST OTHERS DON'T KNOW ABOUT ME: I have fathered several litters out of wedlock, but I think my wife forgives me up in kitty heaven.

MY FAVORITE PHYSICAL ACTIVITIES: Patiently grooming a wonderful queen, and gladly accepting her tongue strokes in return.

MY MOTTO: This, too, shall pass—especially with an extra dose of prune juice with every meal.

Purr-fect!

SEX KITTENS 50

Boing, Boing, Boing!!!

What I'm Looking For: Frisky CAT needs young, attractive CAQ, petites preferred. You: be fun-loving, energetic, sincere. Not having any fun with your boring old humans, with their paper towel tubes and stupid yarn toys? I could be the antidote!

Why You Want To Get To Know Me: I'm fun!!! Why sit around talking about the same old yawn, yawn, yawn, when you could be wrassling and wrecking the house with me? We can bite each other and then run as fast as we can, from one end of the house to the other. I like to play hide-and-seek, and when I find you, you'd better be ready for a little love tackle!

My Ideal Date Includes: We'd head next door, where there's a hyper little terrier who barks at the slightest provocation. We can run back and forth along the fence and make him go hoarse with outrage—and then, when he's exhausted, we can shove the flowerpots off the fence and onto his pointy little head! Just be ready to run if you hear the back door opening....

My Favorite Physical Activities: Sneaking and jumping—and kissing in the dark!!!

My Motto: Life's a mouse on the run— get ready to pounce!!!

SEX
KITTENS
51

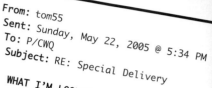

From: tom55
Sent: Sunday, May 22, 2005 @ 5:34 PM
To: P/CWQ
Subject: RE: Special Delivery

WHAT I'M LOOKING FOR: Family-minded CWT seeks P/CWQ, must be fertile with a good mothering instinct and ready to settle down with a loving partner in a good neighborhood and start popping out litters.

WHY YOU WANT TO GET TO KNOW ME: I've got a good job at the post office (that's me packing a box for a customer in the pic), and I'm kind, generous, supportive, and eager to raise my own brood of little whisker-biters. I look forward to playing catch in the backyard with the kits, tossing a mouse back and forth on weekends—just like I always wanted to do with my dad!

WHAT'S IN MY BEDROOM: A lined box I sleep in that has plenty of room for me, you, and our first litter of kittens.

MY IDEAL DATE INCLUDES: We meet at the local docks for a meal of fresh seafood (I know a nice little place), followed by a stroll along the wharf. When it's time to go, I whisk you off to a romantic rooftop, where we make love in the moonlight.

A SECRET MOST OTHERS DON'T KNOW ABOUT ME: I come from a broken home—my daddy was a stray just passing through for the night, and my mom was a catnip addict.

MY MOTTO: Fortune favors the large family.

SEX
KITTENS
52

PERSONALS

DID YOU HEAR THAT SOUND?!

WHAT I'M LOOKING FOR: Fragile CAT needs levelheaded CAQ for soothing companionship. You: be a kind, sensitive, and, above all, SANE queen with a gentle touch.

WHY YOU WANT TO GET TO KNOW ME: I'm a loving, well-educated tom with a Ph.D. in human studies. I have deep insights into the world of *Homo sapiens*, but at a terrible price: After a freak accident at a government lab, I was bitten by a radioactive human child run amok, cursing me with the ability to see dead people. I am now retired and live on a government stipend, unable to sleep.

WHAT I'M READING: *The Invisible Man, Triumph Over Shyness,* and *I'm Normal, You're Normal: Overcoming the Sudden Advent of Mutant Superpowers.*

MY IDEAL DATE INCLUDES: Something low-key and far away from the stress and strain of the outside world. I'd love to curl up next to you in a small dark space somewhere and fall asleep in your paws.

I'M MOST NEUROTIC ABOUT: Running into the ghosts of "dog people"—they're so smug!

SEX KITTENS 53

MY MOTTO: Get that thing away from me.

There's Always Room for Mini Muffins!

WHAT I'M LOOKING FOR: Munchy-prone CAT hungry for P/CAQ with an appetite for romance and snack foods. If the words "Atkins," "The Zone," or "South Beach Diet" are in your vocabulary, you probably don't want to get involved.

WHY YOU WANT TO GET TO KNOW ME: I admit it: I'm a snack-food junkie. I stay fit and healthy, though, with lots of running and climbing, and I've never had a cavity in my life. Couch potatoes bore me, so you should be ready to gnaw on a Fruit Roll-Up one minute, then have a race to the top of the fridge the next.

WHAT I'M READING:
Candyfreak: A Journey Through the Chocolate Underbelly of America, the latest issue of *Cook's Illustrated*, and *The Connoisseur's Guide to American Junk Food*, 7th Ed.

MY DREAM VACATION:
First, we smoke a little catnip in the parking lot, then head into the Little Debbie snack factory and take the tour, culminating in an all-you-can-eat "baked" goods buffet.

MY MOTTO: Everything in life should be made with preservatives—even love muffins!

SEX KITTENS 54

Epicurean Seeks Tasty Dish

From: tom623
Sent: Tuesday, June 7, 2005 @ 10:17 AM
To: CA/WQ
Subject: RE: Epicurean Seeks Tasty Dish

WHAT I'M LOOKING FOR: CAT needs a spicy little CA/WQ to liven up my love life. There's a difference between a sophisticated eater and a finicky one; the latter sort need not apply. All types welcome, but longhaired breeds preferred.

WHY YOU WANT TO GET TO KNOW ME: I like to savor a finely cooked meal, fine wine, and most of all, fine felines with gusto and flair. Your average run-of-the-mill tom can't appreciate the nuanced layers, the delicate bouquet, of a perfectly aged queen in all her glory—I can!

WHAT I'M LISTENING TO/WATCHING: On TV: *Iron Chef, Nigella Bites,* any Discovery Channel oceanography special—mmm-MMMM! The music of Cesaria Evora—they make great tunes to cook by in Cape Verde!

A SECRET MOST OTHERS DON'T KNOW ABOUT ME: I'm a phenylketonuric.

MY MOTTO: "There is no love sincerer than the love of food."

SEX KITTENS 55

Tense? Let Me Work My Magic

WHAT I'M LOOKING FOR: CAT waiting for the right CQ, altered or whole, with a knot in her shoulders and a space in her heart for a sensitive but masculine tom with magic paws. You bring yourself, and I'll bring the scented oil.

WHY YOU WANT TO GET TO KNOW ME: I'm a trained professional cat masseur with three years of experience helping cats of all shapes and sizes find sweet, relaxing release.

WHAT'S IN MY BEDROOM: Dim lighting, sounds of the rain forest, and a deluxe cat massage table.

MY IDEAL DATE INCLUDES: You, me, Barry White on the stereo, edible panties, whipped cream, and a lot of slow, sensual rubbing....

A SECRET MOST OTHERS DON'T KNOW ABOUT ME: I have six toes on my right back paw.

MY MOTTO: The secret to happiness is a thoroughly rubbed muscle.

SEX KITTENS 56

P E R S O N A L S

DESPERATE HOUSEPETS DATING SERVICE

HELL'S ANGEL NEEDS A DEVIL DOLL

WHAT I'M LOOKING FOR:
Cycle-enthusiast CAT in search of CAQ to ride with me down the road of life—or at least to the next road-house. Interest in vintage British motorbikes a plus.

WHY YOU WANT TO GET TO KNOW ME: If you like speed, loud noise, and high-octane good times with a tom who doesn't feel fully dressed without his leather chaps and Stahlhelm, I'm your cat. I'm good with engines and can fix just about anything around the house, too.

WHAT'S IN MY BEDROOM:
Bedrooms are for domestics! I'm king of the road, baby: The pavement is my pillow and the sky is my ceiling. If you're into the soft, toothless lifestyle of a common, overstuffed tabby, you're pumping the wrong gas.

MY IDEAL DATE INCLUDES: I'm all about speed and motion, so first we'd grab a ride on my bike and pop some wheelies. After you feel the wind in your fur, you'll forget all about that old habit of walking everywhere. Then we'd head to my favorite bar, Catfight, and chug some beers.

MY MOTTO: Everything looks better from the saddle of a Triumph.

Call Tonight!

SEX KITTENS 57

Trick or Treat This!

WHAT I'M LOOKING FOR: Refugee CAT, recent victim of a holiday joke gone terribly wrong, now finds himself with new human family and in need of some sweet loving from his own CQ, altered or whole makes no difference. No black cats, please.

WHY YOU WANT TO GET TO KNOW ME: I'm sweet and easygoing. Maybe a tad gullible, too: It all started when the doorbell rang at my old house. A second later, my previous human's teenage son stuffed me into the trick-or-treat sack of a cute little witch who was standing there in the doorway. I didn't really expect the girl to bring me all the way back to her house, but that's what happened. Now I'm staying here permanently, just to make a point.

WHAT'S IN MY BEDROOM: You're looking at it. I'm hoping I get some space of my own, but for now, it looks like I'll be sleeping on the La-Z-Boy.

MY GREATEST AMBITION: To sneak back into my old house one night, creep into the teenage boy's bedroom, claw up his crotch, then pee in his car on my way out. Let's see how date night goes after that!

MY MOTTO: I hate Halloween.

SEX
KITTENS
58

Cantare, Amore

What I'm Looking For: Baritone CWT seeks PWQ for duets, open-mike nights, possible long-term commitment. Must have own tuning fork.

Why You Want To Get To Know Me: I can mew like you've never heard before. I have perfect pitch and write my own, glorious compositions that I will sing to you day and night. I will serenade you until you slake my thirst for your love (actually, I might continue singing throughout the actual act as well...) or until some meddling human interrupts us.

What I'm Listening To:
The collected works of Caruso (Decca), Enrique Iglesias, and Jens Lekman's *When I Said I Wanted To Be Your Dog.*

I'm Most Neurotic About:
Sometimes I have a recurring nightmare that Ursula from the Little Mermaid is stealing my voice, just like she did to Ariel.

My Motto: "Sing! Sing a song! Don't worry that it's not good enough for anyone else to hear. Just sing! Sing a song!"

Pop Artist Seeks Muse

WHAT I'M LOOKING FOR: Artistically inclined PWT seeks beautiful PA/WQ who is comfortable posing in the nude. Rubenesque queens welcome.

WHY YOU WANT TO GET TO KNOW ME: I am quite serious about my career and about my sexual partners. Also, I am at the forefront of the new wave in feline-made pop art. My medium is cat litter, hardened with a special mix of urine and some horrible-smelling stuff I found in a bottle under the kitchen sink. I'm having a show in Black's Alley in April, for which I plan to create a cycle of nude litter portraits —perhaps of you?

WHAT'S IN MY BED-ROOM: It looks like a normal bedroom, but there are dozens of litter boxes with my portraits, landscapes, and still-lifes, and even some examples of my African mask period hidden all over the room. I have to hide them so my owners keep buying me new boxes.

A SECRET MOST OTHERS DON'T KNOW ABOUT ME: I wasted 3 of my lives watching football on TV before I discovered my unique talent.

I'M MOST NEUROTIC ABOUT: My owners raking over my art before my special epoxy has time to set the litter in place.

MY MOTTO: "Art is a jealous mistress."

SEX
KITTENS
60

Cat Burglar Wants to Steal Your Heart

From: tom333
Sent: Wednesday, April 13, 2005 @ 5:34 PM
To: CA/WQ
Subject: RE: Cat Burglar Wants to Steal Your Heart

WHAT I'M LOOKING FOR: Wily CAT wants to partner with an agile, CA/WQ for criminal and romantic capers away from prying eyes. You: be clever, sexy, and not afraid to break the law.

WHY YOU WANT TO GET TO KNOW ME: I'm a master thief, I speak eight languages (including Indo-Siamese), and I like to travel around the world. I go where I want when I want, and nobody can stop me. And besides, living life on the straight-and-narrow is for the dogs.

A SECRET MOST OTHERS DON'T KNOW ABOUT ME: The only time I got caught, it was for stealing anchovy filets from the fridge. I was locked into a cat carrier and dragged to the vet, where the bastard gave me five shots. I was released under my own recognizance within 24 hours, so the sentence seemed light, but ever since then I haven't had any hairballs... you do the math.

MY DREAM VACATION: A month in Venice, where cats rule the city.

MY MOTTO: If stealing hearts is a crime, then I'm America's most wanted!

SEX KITTENS 61

Frisky Grampa Needs Sexy Granny

WHAT I'M LOOKING FOR: No-nonsense, mature CWQ to provide company and romance to an old coot who's still got a lot of piss and vinegar in him. You gotta be unaltered—God gave us this equipment and we ain't getting any younger, so we oughta use it while it still might work.

WHY YOU WANT TO GET TO KNOW ME: I'm a funny elderly fella with an easy laugh, but I'm also a crusty old codger who's set in his ways. So don't come into this relationship thinking you're gonna suddenly get me to try those new fancy-style cat foods, like that wet garbage that comes in cans. If I want my food wet, I'll pour water on it.

MY DREAM VACATION: I don't need a dang vacation. If you like farm life—and who wouldn't?—this is the place to be.

A SECRET MOST OTHERS DON'T KNOW ABOUT ME: Sometimes I need a little help from Viagra. What do you expect at the age of 14? It just works when you want it to? Ha.

MY FAVORITE PHYSICAL ACTIVITIES: Hoofing it down to the General Store to lie on the porch. That's about as physical as I get these days, plus my eyes still work, dagnabit, and there's some mighty fine female felines down Main Street way.

MY MOTTO: If it ain't broke, don't fix it (but if it IS broke, get professional help—that's what Medicare is for, ya idjit!).

SEX KITTENS 62

RAT CIRCUS IMPRESARIO

WHAT I'M LOOKING FOR: Ringmaster of a successful, traveling rodent circus seeks easygoing, physically gifted CA/WQ to be partner in life's most death-defying stunt: a successful relationship. Must not be afraid of heights or mice. Rabies shots a plus.

WHY YOU WANT TO GET TO KNOW ME: I'm the mastermind behind the Greatest Feline Entertainment on Earth! Also, I'm warm, loving, and a self-made cat. I may not be rich, but I am the master of my own destiny, and I'd like to share that destiny with a special queen. Our troupe tours 8 months of the year, so you should have a taste for life on the road.

WHAT'S IN MY BEDROOM: Rat-sized bicycles, brightly colored balance balls, tiny clown outfits, miniature trapeze and nets, and a Radio Flyer wagon for transporting the tent.

WHAT I'M READING/WATCHING: *Circus Fire: A True Story, E Pluribus Barnum: The Great Showman and the Making of U.S. Popular Culture, Freaks.*

MY MOTTO: Step right this way!

Meow!

SEX KITTENS 63

The Good Life

WHAT I'M LOOKING FOR: Wealthy bachelor seeks intelligent, refined PAQ with exquisite taste who appreciates the finer things in life for love, sex, and possibly even long-term commitment. Let me take you to the Côte d'Azur, where I have a sprawling villa nestled in the hills above St. Tropez.

WHY YOU WANT TO GET TO KNOW ME: I'm a generous, warm-hearted, handsome PAT. Did I mention the villa?

WHAT'S IN MY BEDROOM: A huge antique canopy bed, a plush carpet-covered jungle gym, a mahogany scratching post, and sterling silver food and water dishes.

MY IDEAL DATE INCLUDES: We'd go for a walk around the grounds, and I'd catch you our dinner in the koi pond. After our meal we'd sit by the fireplace while my majordomo, François, attended to our every desire. Then we'd move to the bedroom, where I would treat you like the queen you are.

A SECRET MOST OTHERS DON'T KNOW ABOUT ME: My family fortune was made in the slave trade. In the 1920s, my great-great-great-great-great-great-grandfather smuggled thousands of Manx cats into the United States before the traffic in felines was put to an end by the Feds.

MY MOTTO: Pardon me—have you any Grey Poupon?

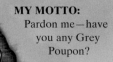

SEX KITTENS 64

40 Acres and a Cat

What I'm Looking For:
Down-home CWT seeks PWQ
to start a big family out
here in the fresh country air.
My ideal queen loves
spending the day outside,
sleeping in tall grass,
chasing grasshoppers, and
raising several litters of
strong, healthy kittens to
carry on the family line.

**Why You Want To
Get To Know Me:**
I'm sturdily built,
I never get sick, and I'm a
rock-solid citizen of this
good Earth. I'm quite
good with my paws, too, even if they are a little rough from all the hard work
it takes to keep the farm going. Depending on how the day's going, I can
whittle toys for the young 'uns or give you a nice back rub after a tough
day in the fields.

What I'm Reading/Listening To: I never miss a Saturday night in front
of the radio listening to Garrison Keillor's *A Prairie Home Companion*,
and I'm a huge fan of the books of James Herriot and Gerald Durrell.
Don't own a TV and don't want one—there'll be no desperate housewives
in my home!

My Motto: It's been a quiet week out here in Lake Mousebegone....

SEX
KITTENS
65

Cubicalist Seeks Escape

WHAT I'M LOOKING FOR: Computer-programmer PAT iso all-natural P/CA queen who thinks "rat race" means fast food, and who doesn't know a thing about IT, Windows XP, or C (or C++). Luddites preferred.

WHY YOU WANT TO GET TO KNOW ME: I'm an ambitious, energetic tom with a good job in a high-paying industry. Still, I'm getting a little sick of the old 9-to-5, so I need to step out with a queen who can really light my fire. Plus, I make awesome nachos.

WHAT I'M READING/WATCHING: I like to collect travel guides and daydream about what life might be like on the road. Currently reading *Status Anxiety*, by Alain de Botton. My favorite movie is *Office Space*, though *Something Wild* is a close runner-up.

I'M MOST NEUROTIC ABOUT:
I have a recurring dream about showing up to a meeting late with food stuck on my whiskers and no fur on.

MY MOTTO:
Something different, something daring, something dangerous.

SEX KITTENS
66

Romantic Rambo

From: tom958
Sent: Tuesday, June 28, 2005 @ 6:11 PM
To: P/CWQ
Subject: RE: Romantic Rambo

WHAT I'M LOOKING FOR: Mildly obsessive, survivalist CWT wants to catch beautiful WQ, pure or cross-bred, and possess her, heart and soul. You: A lawless banana republic at war with itself. Me: A highly trained member of an elite U.S. expeditionary force, inserted within your borders to take out the trash.

WHY YOU WANT TO GET TO KNOW ME: I am a muscular, self-sufficient tom who has completely rejected the human order. I catch my own food, I sleep wherever I want, and I slash first and ask questions later. As my queen, you can rest assured: There won't be a moment that passes when I won't be watching you—while you eat, while you sleep, while you use the bathroom, and so on.

MY IDEAL DATE INCLUDES: I go to your house with binoculars and sit outside your window. I watch you tongue-bathe yourself and get dressed, then pick you up at your cat-door at precisely the appointed time. In fact, I'm outside watching you right now....

A SECRET MOST OTHERS DON'T KNOW ABOUT ME: I have been served with a restraining order three times now, can you believe that?

MY MOTTO: Your lips say, "No," but according to my infrared goggles, your elevated pulse suggests that your heart says, "Love me forever."

SEX KITTENS 67

¡Sì, Chica—Es Muy Picante!

WHAT I'M LOOKING FOR: Sensualist CAT iso P/CAQ who wants a one-way ticket to the realm of the senses. You have an insatiable appetite for hot and spicy lovemaking. Yowlers preferred.

WHY YOU WANT TO GET TO KNOW ME: I'm a red-hot Latin lover with a lot of extra sauce to go around. I'm triple-jointed at two points on my spine, and when it comes to the kitchen of love, I'm a master chef. There's not a spot on my body I can't lick, and I'd love to show you what that translates to in the language of love.

A SECRET MOST OTHERS DON'T KNOW ABOUT ME: One of my former lovers nicknamed my "special friend" *el grande habañero.*

MY MOTTO: I hope you're hungry tonight, *chica,* because *amor* is on the menu and it's a nine-course meal.

Hottie!

SEX KITTENS 68

PERSONALS

LUKE SHYWALKER SEEKS PRINCESS LAY-A

WHAT I'M LOOKING FOR:
Shy, Star Wars–obsessed
CWT iso outgoing CA/WQ
for friendship, conversation,
maybe more. You are
patient with introverts and
like to play 3D holographic
space chess. Dominatrix
a plus.

**WHY YOU WANT TO GET TO
KNOW ME:** I'm a nice guy
with a couple of hang-ups,
but I come from a good
family and have a steady
job (claim surveyor for the

Feline Revenue Service).
I lead a pretty quiet life, but I have an active imagination, and what I've been
imagining lately involves a proud warrior-daughter of the Galactic Federation
dressed in a patent-leather hip boots, teaching me the physics of love at the
end of a laser-whip.

MY IDEAL DATE INCLUDES: After downing a tasty meal of Tattoine Swamp Rat,
we retire to my luxurious hoverbed in Cloud City. After I tell my retainers that
I don't wish to be disturbed, I take out my light saber and you show me the
warm side of the Force.

WHAT I'M READING/LISTENING TO/WATCHING: All of John Williams's
soundtracks are in constant rotation, by my bedside is Frank Herbert's
entire *Dune* cycle, and I have my computer hooked into the
SETI network 24/7 (I know they're out there somewhere!).

MY MOTTO: My mother always said I could be anything I
wanted to when I grew up, as long as I put my mind to it.

SEX
KITTENS
69

Sigma Nu Brothers Seek Queen Gone Wild

WHAT WE'RE LOOKING FOR: Two totally cool Frat cats seek hot CWQ for fun times, no commitments. Must have slammin' body and like to party. Get ready to have an awesome time with a couple of wild and crazy CWT frat brothers!

WHY YOU WANT TO GET TO KNOW US: We're best buds who've lived together since birth, and our freshman year, we started the local branch of Sigma Nu. We have the most awesome parties all the time, like Pimps 'n Hos back in '04; we were dressed as pimps and we looked totally sick! And we both got laid that night. High five!!!

WHAT'S IN OUR BEDROOM: A basketball, a football, a beer bong, a bong bong, boxers with holes in the crotch, empty beer cans, old boxes of pizza, and the *Felines of Aruba Sports Illustrated Swimsuit Issue.*

OUR IDEAL DATE: We, like, meet you at the bar and have nachos grande and burgers and some pitchers. Then we swing back to the house and totally make the beast with three backs!

OUR MOTTO: Go Tigers! Sigma Nu rocks!

SEX KITTENS 70

Pre-Post-Grad Malaise

What I'm Looking For: Pre-doctoral CAT seeks non-academic PA/WQ with a good career. You are unpretentious, sexy, smart and have no unpaid school loans (I'll supply plenty of those, trust me).

Why You Want To Get To Know Me: I'm pretty funny, but I can also be serious when I want to. I'm pursuing my Ph.D. in Roman history (my thesis is on Cato the Elder), which mainly makes me good at cocktail parties but kind of makes my job prospects grim.

What I'm Reading: I'm currently reading *Roman Rodents Reconsidered: Exploring the Rat/Feline Dialectic in Ancient Rome* (a professor on my thesis review committee wrote it, so I kind of have to read it).

A Secret Most Others Don't Know About Me: I smoke a lot of catnip, but maybe that's not such a big deal. I mean, who doesn't, these days? Of course, I spend a lot of time in bed as a result, but then again, that could just be mild depression. I guess that's two secrets....

My Motto: "He approaches nearest to gods who knows how to be silent, even though he is in the right."

Neat Freak Wants Dirty Girl

WHAT I'M LOOKING FOR: Ultra-tidy CAT iso messy CAQ who'll storm into my life like a Tasmanian devil. You can go crazy and let me take care of cleaning up your mess. Go ahead, break the china, shred the furniture, cough hairballs up on the pillows—knock yourself out!

WHY YOU WANT TO GET TO KNOW ME: I am the most fastidious tom you'll ever meet, but I absolutely LOVE a cleaning challenge. I'm happy to be the "Felix" in this odd couple, so if you're sick of being a stereotype, I'm the feline for you. And nothing turns me on more than the sight and smell of a litter box that's filled to overflowing—just let me at it!

WHAT'S IN MY BEDROOM: A perfectly made, spotless bed, a dust-free floor, and a small trashcan where I place all the shed hair (human and feline). Come trash the joint and I just may kiss you on the lips and call you "sweetheart."

A SECRET MOST OTHERS DON'T KNOW ABOUT ME: My mother was a real hard-ass, which my therapist says is the root of my neurosis, but who cares? I'm happy the way I am and I've never had a lover who begrudged me my...germicidal tendencies.

MY MOTTO: An ordered home leads to an ordered mind.

SEX KITTENS 72

Hunky Stud!

Ultra-Marathoner Seeks Training Partner

From: tom888
Sent: Sunday, June 19, 2005 @ 12:47 PM
To: CA/WQ
Subject: Ultra-Marathoner Seeks
Training Partner

WHAT I'M LOOKING FOR: Reformed CWT fattie (that's me in my "before" picture, with my first treadmill) wants to team up with an athletic CA/WQ who likes to run hard and run long. "Big-boned" queens need not apply—I need a girlfriend who can keep up, in the sack and on the road.

WHY YOU WANT TO GET TO KNOW ME: I'm a tom's tom who doesn't get all that pilates and Swiss ball stuff. Our feline ancestors were born to run across the ancient plains, not balance on an inflatable ball or be stretched on a reformer. I lift weights and work my butt off on long runs through the neighborhood and on the treadmill to stay in top shape.

MY IDEAL DATE INCLUDES: Like I said, I don't get into fancy stuff, so I'd take you out to a restaurant with good, honest food, like maybe the house down the street, where they have an ornamental carp pond in the backyard. We don't have to fall into bed on the first date, but I'd at least like to kiss you goodnight at the end.

A SECRET MOST OTHERS DON'T KNOW ABOUT ME: When I was a kitten, my football coach told my mom I had three left feet.

MY MOTTO: Never run from, always run to.

SEX
KITTENS
73

Clothes Horse Wants Arm Candy

From: dam45490
Sent: Tuesday, June 14, 2005 @ 8:46 AM
To: PAQ
Subject: RE: Clothes Horse Wants Arm Candy

WHAT I'M LOOKING FOR: Stylish PAT iso PAQ with great body, into shopping, looking/feeling good, and making her tom the proudest cat on the block. Must be size 8 or smaller, sorry.

WHY YOU WANT TO GET TO KNOW ME: I'm a handsome, healthy tom who's quick to praise when he sees something he likes. I'm proud but not vain (or is it the other way around?). As a self-avowed clothes horse, I want you to look your best, so I'll always be glad to help groom you in all those hard-to-reach spots.

MY IDEAL DATE INCLUDES: We cruise the aisles at Barney's New York, looking for that special outfit. When closing time rolls around, we stow away in a shopping bag until everyone leaves. Then we make love on a shimmery satin item or cashmere dainty; then, before we blissfully pass out from exhaustion, we cough up a couple of hair-balls on the disgraceful off-the-rack eveningwear.

I'M MOST NEUROTIC ABOUT: Sneezing in public.

MY MOTTO: I'm not gay, dammit—just metro.

SANTA CLAWS

WHAT I'M LOOKING FOR: Playful CAT iso P/CAQ with keen eyesight for long games of hide and seek. You: be limber, a fast runner, quiet, and eager to engage in a little personal hunting for fun and pleasure. Remember, I get a reward every time I catch you.

WHY YOU WANT TO GET TO KNOW ME: I'm always ready for a game of chase. I'm playful and imaginative and love to surprise my girlfriend with a sudden leap from a previously empty-looking clothes hamper, or with a paw swipe from under a seemingly innocent pillow.

WHAT I'M READING/WATCHING: Reading: *Harriet the Spy*. Watching: *Get Smart*, *The Avengers*, *Lost*.

MY IDEAL DATE INCLUDES: Well, you'd wait for me and grow more and more annoyed as I didn't show up. But surprise! In a sudden leap, I'd tackle you from the shadows. I was here all along!

MY MOTTO: Run silent, run deep.

Meow!

SEX
KITTENS
75

Peanut Gallery Likes to Watch

WHAT WE'RE LOOKING FOR: We're three old bull toms, all CA, iso a petite PA/WQ with an exhibitionist streak a mile wide, to perform at our private parties. Prefer professional dancers, personal trainers, or prize-winning show cats, but no enthusiastic ameteur will be turned down for an audition.

WHY YOU WANT TO GET TO KNOW US: We're dignified, respectable toms who know how to mind our manners. We won't ask you to do anything you're not comfortable with. We can appreciate your beauty at a distance, marveling at your feminine gifts while keeping our paws to ourselves.

OUR IDEAL DATE INCLUDES: After we've eaten dinner, we'll give you the signal to come in. You'll take your position in the performance area. At your leisure, you'll begin a spell-binding dance of erotic feline sensuality. We'll tuck bills in your collar for particularly creative moves.

A SECRET MOST OTHERS DON'T KNOW ABOUT US: One of us is blind, but he still enjoys the smell of a sexy queen.

OUR MOTTO: The female figure is meant to be worshiped and we are always at the temple.

SEX KITTENS 76

Feline de Sade

What I'm Looking For:
CAT needs a harsh mistress, PA/WQ, to teach me to behave myself. Be a take-charge queen who won't tolerate all the attitude I'm going to throw at you. Must have all claws and not be recently trimmed. Foul-mouthed Persians are especially welcome.

Why You Want To Get To Know Me: I'm a bad, bad, bad, bad tom who's always getting into trouble. I have a horrible temper and a dirty butt, and I need to be punished, NOW. See that mess I made? Go ahead, rub my nose in it. Also, I'm quite handsome underneath the bag.

What's In My Bedroom: Extensive collection of leather diapers, studded collars, and latex masks. I like being shoved in a dirty tube sock when I've been extra naughty.

A Secret Most Others Don't Know About Me: My parents were both on Broadway back in the '90s and died in an audience stampede during a weekend matinee performance of *Cats*.

My Motto: Make me.

SEX KITTENS 77

QUEENS
SEEKING
TOMS

You Can't Run From Love

WHAT I'M LOOKING FOR: Hyperactive CAQ seeks young, athletic CAT with a positive outlook on life and lots of energy. Must take his health seriously. No performance-enhancing drugs (i.e., catnip), please. Sports fan/athlete a big plus.

WHY YOU WANT TO GET TO KNOW ME: I'm a high-energy kitty, and I love sports, especially wrestling and track & field. My day is not complete until I've sprinted from one end of the house to the other several times, which I prefer to do at 2:00 a.m. My friends call me "Pepper" or "Spazz."

WHAT'S IN MY BEDROOM: Very small barbells, a scratch-and-stretch area, and my "training zone" (which includes the bookcase, the headboard, the curtains, and the top of the dresser).

WHAT I'M LISTENING TO: Hoobastank, Incubus, Bush, Alkaline Trio.

MY IDEAL DATE INCLUDES: We'd chase each other through the house like lunatics until we were put outside, and then we'd have a tree-climbing contest. The winner gets a thorough bathing from the loser!

MY MOTTO: Feel the burn!

Purr-fect!

SEX
KITTENS
80

Unwrap My Heart

What I'm Looking For: This PAQ is looking for the CAT with enough curiosity, intelligence, and sensitivity to take the time to discover the Real Me hidden beneath all the layers of protection.

Why You Want To Get To Know Me: I'm a devoted friend and lover—if I believe in you, I'll be yours forever. I'm very spiritual and can spend hours staring out the window, pondering life's mysteries—or just spacing out. I can be inscrutable, but I long for the tom who can figure me out.

What I'm Listening To/Watching: Watching: *Deadwood, 24, Desperate Housewives*, the Lifetime Channel. Currently listening to: Aimee Mann, anything by Joni Mitchell.

I'm Most Neurotic About: My looks. I know I'm a fairly attractive cat, but I was entered in a cat show once and it scarred me for life.

A Secret Most Others Don't Know About Me: I once hid in a cake for my ex-boyfriend's birthday. It took weeks to get all the frosting out of my fur.

My Motto: Oscar Wilde said it best: "The final mystery is oneself."

SEX KITTENS 81

Make Me Purr

From: queen202
Sent: Sunday, June 7, 2005 @ 4:43 PM
To: CAT
Subject: RE: Make Me Purr

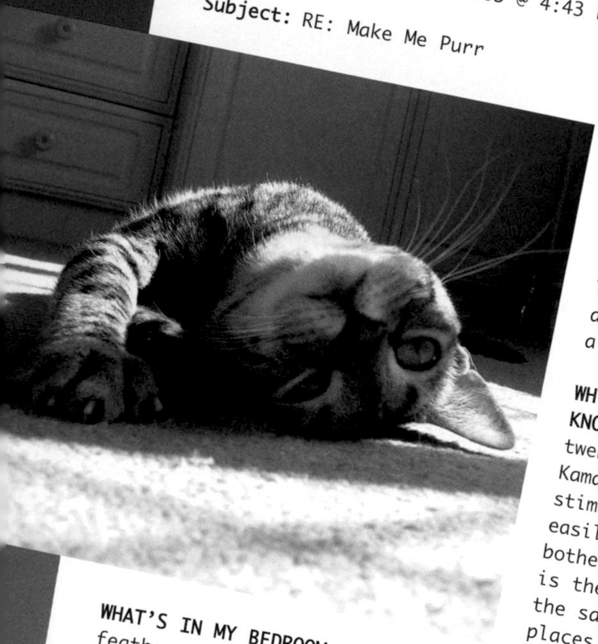

WHAT I'M LOOKING FOR: CWQ seeks any CAT, neutered a must, ready to spend quality time with a lithe, limber minx who's up for a little fun. (Full disclosure: not really a minx.)

WHY YOU WANT TO GET TO KNOW ME: I know more than twenty positions from the Kama Sutra. I'm easily stimulated. But I'm also easily bored, so don't bother if your idea of love is the same position, with the same claws in the same places, every time.

WHAT'S IN MY BEDROOM: A copy of *Teach Yourself Tantric Sex*; a feather boa; a bowl of little nibbly things for you to feed me as we make cosmic, passionate love.

A SECRET MOST OTHERS DON'T KNOW ABOUT ME: I can balance on the tip of my tail.

MY MOTTO: You can hurry love, but why would you want to?

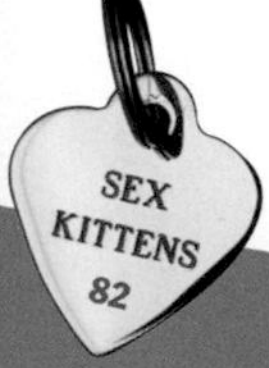

SEX
KITTENS
82

PERSONAL

BORN EXPLORER SEEKS ADVENTURES OF THE HEART

WHAT I'M LOOKING FOR: CAQ seeks fellow traveler, P/CAT, who longs to get out and explore the great outdoors with a partner. I'm a spunky, happy-go-lucky kitty. You: be athletic; eager for new experiences; not too picky about food, cleanliness, or sleeping situation.

WHY YOU WANT TO GET TO KNOW ME: I'm ready to grab life by the neck and shake it until it sprays blood and stops moving. I'm smart, friendly, and fearless.

WHAT'S IN MY BEDROOM: Nothing but dishes of food and water! I like to keep things portable—some day they'll leave that door open....

WHAT I'M READING/WATCHING: Watching: I watch *Milo & Otis* and the *Babe* movies about once a week. I also enjoy *Kitty Safari* videos featuring ducks or chipmunks. My favorite books are *Charlotte's Web* and *Mrs. Frisby and the Rats of N.I.M.H. Animal Farm* cracks me up, too.

MY MOTTO: The world is my litter box!

SEX KITTENS 83

I Want to Show You the Real Me

WHAT I'M LOOKING FOR: PWQ seeks PWT with similar background, preferably a veteran of the pageant circuit who knows what it's like to be a showcat for most of your youth. We both know looks are not truly important—what matters is what's in your heart. Be gentle, understanding, and a good lover.

WHY YOU WANT TO GET TO KNOW ME: I'm a good listener and I'm not the type to get jealous easily. I want to raise a beautiful, happy family with a tom who won't leave me for the next raised tail as soon as we're through making love. I'm ready to put the pageant life behind me and focus on what's real in this world: love, companionship, and family.

WHAT'S IN MY BEDROOM: Several ribbons from past shows; framed professional photographs of me at different ages. My pedigree is on one wall—that's particularly embarrassing to me. My person makes most of the decorating choices.

I'M MOST NEUROTIC ABOUT: Hairbrushes and ribbons.

MY MOTTO: Beauty is only skin deep.

SEX KITTENS 84

Indoor Cat Seeking Same

From: queen6454
Sent: Thursday, June 16, 2005
@ 8:11 AM
To: PAD
Subject: RE: Indoor Cat
Seeking Same

WHAT I'M LOOKING FOR: Looking for nap-loving tom who is willing to try new surfaces. I enjoy sleeping on everything—not just beds, couches, and windowsills, but crossword puzzles, stereos, remote controls, jewelry boxes, refrigerators, dinner plates—I'll try anything once.

WHY YOU WANT TO GET TO KNOW ME: I can sleep in any position and I always look (darn cute) doing it.

WHAT'S IN MY BEDROOM: Lots of bags and boxes my humans forgot about long ago, each perfectly seasoned with a fluffy coating of my spare fur.

MY FAVORITE PHYSICAL ACTIVITIES: Stretching out on flat surfaces, curling into small ones.

I'M MOST NEUROTIC ABOUT: Not being allowed to sleep on something (my humans always throw me off the stove); being woken up too early (like before noon).

MY MOTTO: Lay on any and all surfaces.

SEX
KITTENS
85

A Mystery Wrapped in an Enigma, Then Hidden in a Bag

WHAT I'M LOOKING FOR: I'm a PAQ looking for a self-assured, inquisitive P/CAT who knows what he wants and pursues it. I'm not an easy catch—my tom needs to try hard to keep my interest, and be able to deliver on his promises. At the same time, you should know when a hiss means a hiss and back off.

WHY YOU WANT TO GET TO KNOW ME: I'm attractive but very shy—I need a lot of loving to be coaxed out of my shell. But if you get past that, I can be a tiger! I love silent strolls in the night after everyone else is asleep.

WHAT I'M READING/LISTENING TO/WATCHING: On TV: *Lost*. Reading: *Wuthering Heights*. Listening to: Astor Piazolla. I love to tango—but only when no one's watching, of course.

A SECRET MOST OTHERS DON'T KNOW ABOUT ME: I ate the neighbor's canary that escaped last summer.

I'M MOST NEUROTIC ABOUT: Keeping my white hair clean.

MY MOTTO: A girl should never share all of her secrets.

Meow!

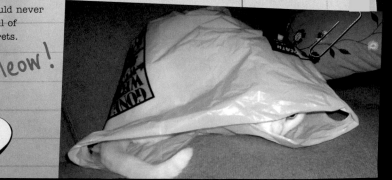

SEX KITTENS 86

It's What's Inside That Counts

What I'm Looking For: I'm a fun-loving, shorthaired queen with an open heart and a taste for the exotic. You are self-confident, comfortable in your own fur, and mild mannered. Career nappers a plus.

Why You Want To Get To Know Me: I'm smart and funny, very clean, and I have a lot of love to give. Access to premium, moist cat food 24/7 is part of the deal. You love old movies, especially romantic comedies starring Cary Grant. Can't have babies and don't mind at all. Very tenderhearted—my feelings bruise easily, so no cruel cats, please.

What I'm Reading/Listening To/Watching: Listening to: anything by Mel Tormé or Shirley Horn. On TV: *Jeopardy!* Reading: I love Helen Fielding's *Bridget Jones* books.

What's In My Bedroom: I keep a very tidy room. For one thing, you'll be hard-pressed to find a single hair in my bed. I also have a collection of special creams and lotions for my skin, and a sweater for chilly days. Finally, there is my cherished blankie, which I'm willing to share with the right guy.

A Secret Most Others Don't Know About Me: You probably won't notice, but I'm actually hairless.

My Motto: Hair is overrated.

SEX KITTENS 87

I Have a Flair for the Dramatic

From: queen62311
Sent: Tuesday, June 28, 2005 @ 3:34 PM
To: CW/AT
Subject: RE: I Have a Flair for the Dramatic

WHAT I'M LOOKING FOR: CWQ seeks CW/AT who can play leading man to my leading lady. You should recognize and respect real talent, and not be tempted by every high-tailed sleek-coated bumpkin fresh off the bus.

WHY YOU WANT TO GET TO KNOW ME: I'm independent, soulful, and artistic. I was an understudy for the original run of *Cats* on Broadway and I had a bit part in *Dr. Doolittle*. My rendition of "Send in the Clowns" was hailed as "unique"—there wasn't a dry eye in the house!

WHAT I'M LISTENING TO/WATCHING: I adore *Yentl* and *Sunset Boulevard* and I love listening to Barbra Streisand.

WHAT'S IN MY BEDROOM: Stacks of scripts from my agent to review; a chaise longue; my collection of cigarette holders (I gave up smoking years ago; bad for the complexion).

MY DREAM VACATION: I would love to visit Egypt—land of our royal fore-felines—and cruise the Nile in a private felucca.

A SECRET MOST OTHERS DON'T KNOW ABOUT ME: Last year I finally gave in and started getting Botox treatments.

MY MOTTO: I'm ready for my close-up.

SEX KITTENS
88

PERSONALS

UNREFORMED TV JUNKIE SEEKS ENABLER

WHAT I'M LOOKING FOR: CAQ seeks another P/CAT like me who'd rather see what's on the idiot box than look out the window. (Make the birds outside vote each other off the tree, and then we'll talk.) You be attractive, intelligent, able to hold your own in a conversation about the careers of '80s sitcom stars. However, social misfits or Kimmy Gibbler types need not apply.

WHY YOU WANT TO GET TO KNOW ME: I'm fun to be around and I have a great sense of humor. Plus I don't talk when the TV is on. I know how to use a remote. I Tivo Animal Planet daily, especially the one about animal stunts and bloopers.

MY IDEAL DATE INCLUDES: I have the entire current season of *24* saved to my Tivo. We would each open a can of cat food—I keep several varieties in stock—and settle in for a Kiefer marathon.

I'M MOST NEUROTIC ABOUT: Being put outside for "fresh air" when I'm trying to watch TV. Someone changing channels when I'm watching TV.

WHAT I'M WATCHING: I Tivo *The Amazing Race*, *Fat Actress*, *The L Word*, *Survivor*, *The Apprentice*, and any *Seinfeld*, *Simpsons*, or *Full House* reruns I can find.

MY MOTTO: Always make sure you have spare batteries.

SEX KITTENS 89

Rapunzel Seeks Her Knight

WHAT I'M LOOKING FOR: CWQ needs knight in shining armor to rescue me! All of my friends are already married with kittens. I'm tired of watching soap operas and not having a romance of my own. I need a CWT who's romantic, passionate, sensitive, and very masculine.

WHY YOU WANT TO GET TO KNOW ME: I'm ready for commitment. In fact, I already have a wedding gown; my colors will be orange and black. My daddy gave me a dowry when I turned 2 and if you're the lucky man, it's all yours. I'm still attractive for my age, but I ain't gettin' any younger....

WHAT'S IN MY BEDROOM: Souvenirs from the day-trips I used to take with my friends before they all got married. China patterns from Bloomingdale's. Copies of *Modern Bride* dating back to 1995. A copy of *The Rules* and *He's Just Not That Into You*.

MY IDEAL DATE INCLUDES: We discuss our future over wine and vole. We decide how many bridesmaids and groomsmen we want, where we'll go for our honeymoon, and how many litters we want. NO Vegas quickie.

MY MOTTO: I just know you're out there somewhere.

SEX
KITTENS
90

Need a Good Businessman

From: queen12
Sent: Friday, June 3, 2005 @ 8:25 AM
To: C/PWT
Subject: RE: Need a Good Businessman

WHAT I'M LOOKING FOR: CAQ iso experienced pimp. I've been in the trade for only a few months and I need some help scoring clients. Am willing to give 50% of my earnings in exchange for a place to sleep and some flea medicine.

WHY YOU WANT TO GET TO KNOW ME: I've got some good skills and I never cough up hairballs.

WHAT'S IN MY BEDROOM: Well, in my box here I've got some wadded-up newspaper, an empty paper cup, a rat tail, and the wrapper from a candy bar.

MY DREAM VACATION: I would love to wander into one of those big pet superstores and be locked in overnight. I'd play with the toys, try out every bed in the building, and have a little fun taunting the fish.

A SECRET MOST OTHERS DON'T KNOW ABOUT ME: My mama taught me everything I know.

MY MOTTO: Follow the red light.

SEX
KITTENS
91

Student of the Heart Seeks Study Partner

WHAT I'M LOOKING FOR: PAQ needs PA/WT, between 1 and 2 years old, for one-on-one tutorials in "math and science." Hotties only, please.

WHY YOU WANT TO GET TO KNOW ME: My mom thinks I need help with school, so I told her I'd find a tutor. I'm not stupid, I just think school is, like, for the birds. I'd much rather spend my time going to the park and meeting cute toms—like you. Hot math geeks, this is your big chance!

A SECRET MOST OTHERS DON'T KNOW ABOUT ME: I was a virgin until I was 9 months old.

I'M MOST NEUROTIC ABOUT: Making the cheerleading squad and, like, keeping up my reputation as the hottest kit in school.

WHAT I'M READING/LISTENING TO/WATCHING: *Heathers, Mean Girls, Girls Just Wanna Have Fun, Dirty Dancing.* I love Pink, No Doubt, and Blink-182. Reading is for nerds.

MY MOTTO:
Like, what's
a motto?

Hottie!

SEX
KITTENS
92

Looking for Real American Beefcake

What I'm Looking For: PWQ wants successful American P/CW/A tom who can show me how to be real American queen.

Why You Want To Get To Know Me: I am exotic feline from Ukraine whose coat is as black and silky as the night. I make any deserving tom a very happy cat. I want start large family as soon as possible.

What's In My Bedroom: Lots of makeup and clothing, picture of Anna Kournikova, back issues of *Pravda*.

My Ideal Date Includes: I want make you happy, so for date I want to be anything you want. I am very skilled at giving baths. I will let you eat my food. I can be pillow for you. And maybe you can teach me words to "Star Spangled Banner"? Still, a tin of caviar would not be turned down.

A Secret Most Others Don't Know About Me: I was part of underground resistance during Cold War.

My Motto: It is an old Ukrainian proverb: "Even ugly cats are not so ugly when viewed with love."

SEX
KITTENS
93

Jungle Beast Under House Arrest

From: queen006
Sent: Tuesday, June 14, 2005 @ 11:13 AM
To: P/CWT
Subject: RE: Jungle Beast Under House Arrest

WHAT I'M LOOKING FOR: Me: oversexed CAQ. You: wild and crazy, confident P/CWT who wants to have fun. Not looking for anything long-term—just be sane, gentle (but not too gentle), and ready to get back to nature. Prefer large toms (over 15 pounds).

WHY YOU WANT TO GET TO KNOW ME: I'm feisty, frisky, flirty, and ferocious! I've been known to send inexperienced toms running back to their momma's teats, so you'd better know what you like and have a plan to get it.

WHAT'S IN MY BEDROOM: Lots of fur that isn't mine. An unmade bed. Bits of catnip (I have no idea where it came from, I swear). Quite possibly a neighborhood tom "visiting" me for the afternoon. Don't like it? That's your problem.

MY IDEAL DATE INCLUDES: Hot cat-on-cat action, and not much else.

I'M MOST NEUROTIC ABOUT: I know that technically I can't, but I always have nightmares where I give birth to a litter of ten or twelve kittens, all of different breeds.

My motto: You can stray with a spay!

SEX KITTENS 94

CAN YOU HANDLE MY BA-DONKA-DONK?

WHAT I'M LOOKING FOR: CAQ needs an affectionate CAT with a big appetite who's eager to treat this plus-size lady like the queen that she is. Must love to get crazy. Should like to treat his queen to a night on the town, not run off prowling without her.

WHY YOU WANT TO GET TO KNOW ME: I've got love to spare and I enjoy life. I like to spend the night out having fun and getting into trouble, and then spend the day sleeping it off while everyone is at work. Sound like your idea of fun? Then hit me up.

WHAT I'M READING/LISTENING TO/WATCHING: Gwen Stefani's "Hollaback Girl" and Sir-Mix-A-Lot's "Baby Got Back." I read a lot of magazines, like *US Weekly* and *Cosmo*. I watch anything on E! and I love the *Ricki Lake Show*.

WHAT'S IN MY BEDROOM: A big-ass bed that's tricked out with satin pillows and a down comforter. Lots of beads that I got in New Orleans during Mardi Gras in '99. A copy of the *Felines Gone Wild* video I was in.

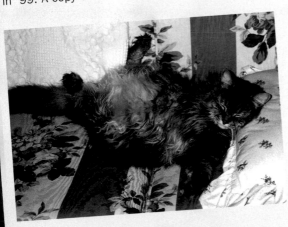

MY FAVORITE PHYSICAL ACTIVITIES: Dancing, getting freaky with the other cats in the neighborhood, generally raising hell.

MY MOTTO: Let's get this party started!

Meow!

SEX KITTENS 95

Huntress Needs Prey

WHAT I'M LOOKING FOR: A wily tom who can break me out of this prison and whisk me off to a place where I can scratch whatever I want, whenever I want, and catch real squirrels. You should be a risk-taker who's not afraid to attack humans if it means getting me outta here and into my new forest home.

WHY YOU WANT TO GET TO KNOW ME: I'm tough, I'm smart, and I'm a born leader. And I'm pretty darn cute, too. Dominant toms who want to control me need not apply.

WHAT I'M READING/ WATCHING: Reading: *The Big Book of Adventure Travel, 1,000 Places to See Before You Die.* TV: *Crocodile Hunter, Wildboyz.*

A SECRET MOST OTHERS DON'T KNOW ABOUT ME: I like playing with ribbons. What can I say? They're irresistible!

MY MOTTO: As Amelia Earhart once said, "Adventure is worthwhile in itself."

SEX KITTENS 96

I Deserve a Love Promotion

From: queen10101
Sent: Sunday, July 3, 2005 @ 8:39 PM
To: CW/AT
Subject: RE: I Deserve a Love Promotion

WHAT I'M LOOKING FOR: CAQ looking for sensible but fun CW/AT with his head on his shoulders—no scorekeepers or young breed-and-flee tomcats, please. You have your own home, a career, realistic plans for the future, and a place in your life for a kitty like me.

WHY YOU WANT TO GET TO KNOW ME: Recovering workaholic who has trouble knowing when to quit. On the plus side, this is how I act in the bedroom, too! Absolutely not momma-cat material. Smart, sophisticated, enjoys the finer things in life.

WHAT I'M READING: *The Wall Street Journal*, *Freakonomics*.

WHAT'S IN MY BEDROOM: A stack of papers I've been meaning to get through but just haven't had the time; a grande liver frappuccino.

A SECRET MOST OTHERS DON'T KNOW ABOUT ME: I can finish the entire Saturday *New York Times* crossword puzzle.

MY MOTTO: Hard work pays off—with hard play.

SEX KITTENS 97

Free Spirit Seeks Same

What I'm Looking For: CAQ seeks CAT who is frisky, wise, artistic, sexy, deep, progressive, and not materialistic. Those who enjoy the music of the Grateful Dead and Phish are encouraged to respond, as well as those who understand the powers of certain mushrooms.

Why You Want To Get To Know Me:
I'm a laid-back momma who followed the Dead for three years. Jerry Garcia scratched me behind my ears and it gave me mystical powers. I only eat organic food and I make a mean grilled cheese and tuna sandwich on the hood of a car.

My Ideal Date Includes: We'd go dig up some of those tasty 'shrooms I discovered in the field behind my house, then spend the afternoon playing with the feather-on-a-stick.

A Secret Most Others Don't Know About Me: I used to be an exotic dancer.

My Motto: Keep on truckin'.

SEXY FELINE MACHINE !

SEX KITTENS 98

Give In to Your Darkest Desires

WHAT I'M LOOKING FOR: PWQ desires PWT to be my sex slave. You must be fit, clean, and eager to obey commands. You should also be prepared to succumb to collars and leashes.

WHY YOU WANT TO GET TO KNOW ME: Because your life of ease—eating and sleeping whenever you want, being coddled and spoiled rotten—has begun to bore you. You crave a mistress who can bring discipline and meaning to your humdrum existence, who will make you feel alive—really alive!

WHAT'S IN MY BEDROOM: A cat-o-nine-tails and a flyswatter with your name on it.

MY IDEAL DATE INCLUDES: Licking. First, I give you a lickin'—with the flyswatter! Then you give me one—a head-to-tail bath, that is.

WHAT I'M READING/ LISTENING TO/WATCHING: Reading: *Venus in Furs*, by Leopold Von Sacher-Masoch, *The Story of O*, by Pauline Reage. Listening to: Verdi, the Velvet Underground, the Violent Femmes. Watching: *La Dolce Vita*, *The Secretary*.

MY MOTTO: Discipline and punish.

SEX KITTENS 99

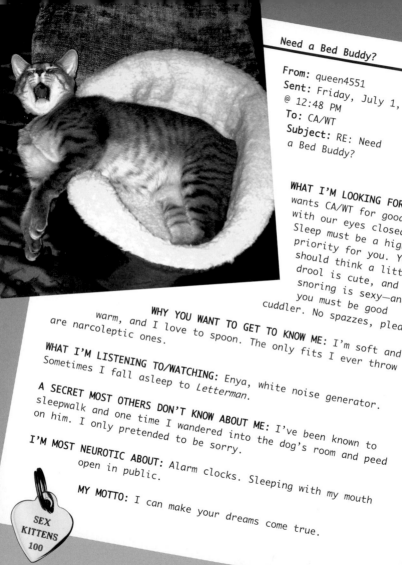

Need a Bed Buddy?

From: queen4551
Sent: Friday, July 1, 2005 @ 12:48 PM
To: CA/WT
Subject: RE: Need a Bed Buddy?

WHAT I'M LOOKING FOR: CAQ wants CA/WT for good times with our eyes closed. Sleep must be a high priority for you. You should think a little drool is cute, and snoring is sexy—and you must be good cuddler. No spazzes, please.

WHY YOU WANT TO GET TO KNOW ME: I'm soft and warm, and I love to spoon. The only fits I ever throw are narcoleptic ones.

WHAT I'M LISTENING TO/WATCHING: Enya, white noise generator. Sometimes I fall asleep to Letterman.

A SECRET MOST OTHERS DON'T KNOW ABOUT ME: I've been known to sleepwalk and one time I wandered into the dog's room and peed on him. I only pretended to be sorry.

I'M MOST NEUROTIC ABOUT: Alarm clocks. Sleeping with my mouth open in public.

MY MOTTO: I can make your dreams come true.

SEX KITTENS 100

P E R S O N A L

EXPERIENCED STOWAWAY WILL SNEAK INTO YOUR HEART

WHAT I'M LOOKING FOR: CWQ seeks world-wise CWT for a little international naughtiness. Must be a member of the "mile-high club." Jetlagged toms need not apply.

WHY YOU WANT TO GET TO KNOW ME: I love to travel, so I don't mind a long-distance relationship. I will respect your freedom; I'm not looking to start a litter of kittens any time soon. I can say "lick me" in four different languages.

WHAT I'M READING/LISTENING TO: Reading: *Travel & Leisure* magazine; *Under the Tuscan Sun*, by Frances Mayes; *How Proust Can Change Your Life*, by Alain de Botton. I love Serge Gainsbourg and Paolo Conti.

I'M MOST NEUROTIC ABOUT: Airport luggage carousels; using public litter boxes in foreign countries.

MY MOTTO: *Voulez-vous couchez avec moi?*

Purr-fect!

SEX
KITTENS
101

Epicurious? Epicarnal!

WHAT I'M LOOKING FOR: Dashing CWT who enjoys the erotic aspects of food, for cooking classes, dining out, kitchen quickies. Any tom who understands the sensual potential of oysters, strawberries, almonds, garlic, figs, or other aphrodisiacs is in for a night of arousal and excitement. Philistines, kindly take your business elsewhere.

WHY YOU WANT TO GET TO KNOW ME: I'm a sophisticated CW calico who seriously knows her way around the kitchen. I have a knack for mixing sex and food and am perfectly capable of cooking you a meal that will make your libido boil over.

WHAT'S IN MY BEDROOM: Well-thumbed first edition of *Mastering the Art of French Cooking*, by Julia Child, chocolate body paint, edible panties, and some honey.

A SECRET MOST OTHERS DON'T KNOW ABOUT ME: Oysters Rockefeller makes my tail stick straight up in the air.

MY MOTTO: Fon-do me, lover boy!

SEX KITTENS 102

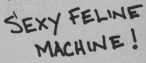

SEXY FELINE MACHINE!

Dormouse Seeks Mad Catter

From: queen7755
Sent: Saturday, July 16, 2005 @ 3:00 PM
To: PWT
Subject: RE: Dormouse Seeks Mad Catter

WHAT I'M LOOKING FOR: Shy young CAQ iso kooky PWT for colorful adventures down the rabbit hole. You are an honest knight with the best of intentions and no STDs.

WHY YOU WANT TO GET TO KNOW ME: I'm a bashful queen with a vivid interior life who needs a real-life lunatic to add a little color to my surroundings. I'm petite and athletic, and my favorite place to sleep is between the sugar bowl and the soup tureen.

BEST/WORST/BIGGEST LIE I EVER TOLD: I once informed a tom I met through a dating service that I had chronic diarrhea and couldn't leave the litter box. I felt like a jerk, but he was really gross.

I'M MOST NEUROTIC ABOUT: My father was polydactyl, and I'm afraid that if I ever have kittens, they may have 6 or 7 toes on each foot as a result.

MY MOTTO: "The time has come, the kitten said, to speak of many things: Of balls of yarn and litter boxes, and feline ding-a-lings."

SEX KITTENS 103

Domestic Goddess Needs Pampering

WHAT I'M LOOKING FOR: Brawny PWT who doesn't feel whole unless he's tongue-bathing a sexy, larger-than-life queen who's sweet as a marshmallow during the day and salty as a sailor at night. My ideal tom has a big appetite, and can handle a gal who knows what she likes.

WHY YOU WANT TO GET TO KNOW ME: As you can see, I have Rubenesque proportions, and you'll have to take my word that my appetites are not only of the Cat Chow variety. Plus, I'm the Martha Stewart of the feline world: Give me a few hours with your broomstick and you'll never look at housework the same way again.

MY IDEAL DATE INCLUDES: You show up hungry and well-rested ('cause it's gonna be a long night). I meet you at the door wearing nothing but a French maid's apron. After a lavish home-cooked meal, I go to work with my feather duster while you watch.

A SECRET MOST OTHERS DON'T KNOW ABOUT ME IS: My belly is very ticklish.

MY MOTTO: We're gonna have a good time tonight— I'd bet my Swiffer on it!

Hottie!

SEX KITTENS 104

Childless Divorcée Seeks Reversal of Fortune

What I'm Looking For: Wonderful, charming P/CWT in the Cary Grant mold who's ready to start a family with this loving, generous queen. You must love kittens and be ready to do more than breed and run. My first husband told me he wanted kittens, and the next day he came home fixed! He claimed the humans forced him, but I remain skeptical (why him and not me, for instance?).

Why You Want To Get To Know Me: I am a still-quite-young PWQ, and many of my friends tell me I'm quite attractive. More importantly, I know I will make a great mother and wife, and I'm looking forward to meeting the tom who will give me the chance to prove it.

What I'm Reading: What to Expect When You're Expecting, Dr. Spock's Baby and Child Care, old issues of Parent magazine.

I'm Most Neurotic About: Not living long enough to see my great-great-great-grandchildren.

My Motto: Let's make ours an affair to remember!

SEX KITTENS 105

Ptooey! on Love

From: queen911
Sent: Monday, July 3, 2005 @ 10:11 AM
To: PWD
Subject: RE: Ptooey! on Love

WHAT I'M LOOKING FOR: A PAT who's tired of playing games and who's sick of "the rules." You are unconventionally handsome, intelligent in an eccentric way, and employed (that's one rule mama doesn't break—sorry, deadbeat toms).

WHY YOU WANT TO GET TO KNOW ME: I'm a CAQ with a long history of queen-meets-tom, queen-falls-in-love, tom-turns-out-not-to-be-able-to-use-the-phone-much-less-cover-up-his-own-litter-box-mess relationships. How about working with me to establish a new paradigm? I can't promise you everything you ever wanted, but I can give you a comfy bed, a sympathetic ear, and devoted companionship.

WHAT I'M READING/WATCHING: My favorite books are A Confederacy of Dunces and The Hitchhiker's Guide to the Galaxy. I often watch The Daily Show and competitive bass fishing on ESPN2.

A SECRET MOST OTHERS DON'T KNOW ABOUT ME: I was adopted from an animal test facility.

MY MOTTO: If I had wanted a conventional life, I would be chasing rodents and licking myself where the sun don't shine.

SEX KITTENS 106

LIFE OF THE PARTY

WHAT I'M LOOKING FOR: I need to find a high-energy CAT who wants to sleep all day and party all night. I need a regular Bukowski—any tomfriend of mine short of those standards is going to suffer premature liver failure. Sissies can go scratch.

WHY YOU WANT TO GET TO KNOW ME: This CAQ is no girly girl. I like to hang out with the fellas, and I can drink most of them under the table. I'll try anything once, as long as I've got a few brews in me. And if I'm drunk enough, any date with me (including the very first) could end in an impromptu striptease.

MY IDEAL DATE INCLUDES: Trolling through the backyards on the other side of the alley behind the 7-Eleven, licking old beer bottles and smoking cigarette butts. Then we'd head to the warehouse district to chase rats and fight for money.

MY FAVORITE PHYSICAL ACTIVITIES: Keg stands, riding the mechanical bull at my favorite bar, and pole-dancing.

MY MOTTO: You think I look funny wearing this thing?! Before you laugh too hard, you better think about how funny it's gonna be when I cram it up your cornhole, tough guy!

SEX KITTEN
107

Simmering for Attention

WHAT I'M LOOKING FOR: Culinary CAQ requests the attentions of a CAT who's a bit of a gourmand. Must have a taste for elaborate, multi-course meals (especially when love is on the menu). Finicky eaters need not apply.

WHY YOU WANT TO GET TO KNOW ME: I'm a successful pastry chef with a thriving catering business. And I've been through three marriages already, so I tend to cut to the chase. Also, I can be a bit bossy, so don't get your tail all in a fluff when I tell you which bowl to use when I need a little extra whipped cream.

WHAT I'M LISTENING TO/WATCHING: On TV: *Nigella Bites* (you can say that again!), *Cooking Under Fire*; I listen to Blue Oyster Cult when I cook, it relaxes me.

MY IDEAL DATE INCLUDES: We travel by train to the lovely grounds of the Culinary Institute of America, where I got my formal training, for a meal prepared and served by the current crop of students. I show you where I lived (not pretty—I had to catch rats to put myself through school), then we retire to a lovely B&B in the area for a nightcap and perfectly spiced lovemaking.

MY MOTTO: Let's just get it out of the way up front—it's the damn copper bowl.

Call Tonight!

SEX KITTENS 108

Spoiled Rotten

From: queen95678
Sent: Tuesday, July 19, 2005
@ 9:49 AM
To: PWT
Subject: RE: Spoiled Rotten

WHAT I'M LOOKING FOR: I'm a PWQ who needs, like, a butler. You: a PWT who's willing to pre-taste my food, warm up my bed for me, scratch litter over my droppings, and do whatever it takes to make sure this gorgeous coat stays clean and fresh. Dumpster-divers, go home.

WHY YOU WANT TO GET TO KNOW ME: Because I'm so balanced: five pounds of adorable and two pounds of cute! Because people can't be in the same room with me without either getting jealous (hello, girls) or falling in love (hello, gents).

WHAT'S IN MY BEDROOM: Brushes, ribbons, an ionic blow-dryer, closet full of designer collars, and a perfectly kept little bed in the shape of a ladybug.

MY IDEAL DATE INCLUDES: You arrive at my door with your paws full of presents. After we gingerly and briefly make love (a bit of a nasty business, I hope you agree), you massage my paws until I fall asleep. When I wake up, a cup of coffee is waiting with two freshly prepared eggs on the side (with little chicks just poking out of the shells).

I'M MOST NEUROTIC ABOUT: Dreadlocks forming in my coat.

MY MOTTO: Brush me! Now leave!

SEX
KITTENS
109

Love from Above!

WHAT I'M LOOKING FOR: Sneaky CWQ on the prowl for a randy, full-bodied CWT to attack with love bites all night long. You: be strong, between one and four years old, and a good sport. 'Fraidy cats need not apply.

WHY YOU WANT TO GET TO KNOW ME: Underneath this adorable exterior is a savage beast, waiting to feast on your sinewy tom-cat body! I'll work you over like a piece of carpet-covered 4X4 and teach you the meaning of "respect."

MY IDEAL DATE INCLUDES: You come over, but I'm nowhere to be found—you pick up my scent, but then find that it mysteriously disappears. As dusk approaches, you begin to wonder—did I leave? Has something happened? You hear a small cracking noise behind you. From my hiding place, I watch your ears flatten as you struggle to keep your cool. Oh, it's just a leaf. And when the game of cat-and-cat becomes unbearable— slam! The full weight of my white-hot feline vitality pins you momentarily to the earth! You twist away, and suddenly you're on top of me....

A SECRET MOST OTHERS DON'T KNOW ABOUT ME: I was the runt of my litter.

MY MOTTO: Love hurts, and that's a good thing.

SEX
KITTENS
110

Tommy Blue, Where Are You?

What I'm Looking For: Rock-hard P/CAT in uniform. Toms in the armed forces, police, or fire-fighters, I want YOU! There's nothing that turns me on more than a crisp, clean uniform on a take-charge kind of guy.

Why You Want To Get To Know Me: I'm a full-bodied CAQ with generous hips and a sincere desire to please. I have a temper when it comes to injustice or pettiness, but I follow directions well and I love role-playing. I have a few uniforms of my own you might like to see, including a pair of thigh-high, white go-go boots (that's the entire outfit, if you see what I mean).

My Ideal Date Includes: Well, that all depends on what uniform you're wearing. Here's an idea: If you're a cop, you break down my door and tell me to put my paws up. You do a full body search. Suddenly, the case takes a turn for the better....

A Secret Most Others Don't Know About Me: My father was a fire-cat with Ladder Company 39, in Columbus, Ohio.

My Motto: I love a tom in a uniform.

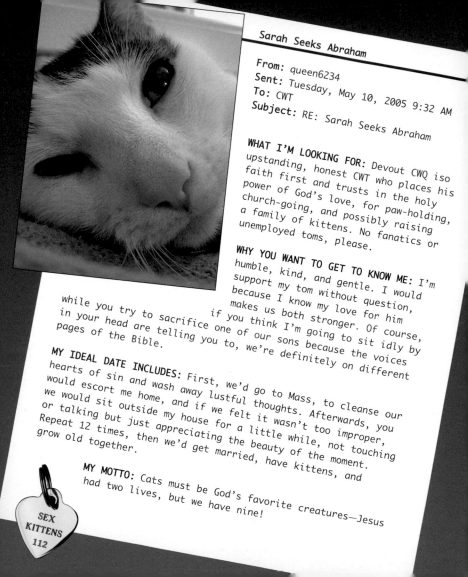

Sarah Seeks Abraham

From: queen6234
Sent: Tuesday, May 10, 2005 9:32 AM
To: CWT
Subject: RE: Sarah Seeks Abraham

WHAT I'M LOOKING FOR: Devout CWQ iso upstanding, honest CWT who places his faith first and trusts in the holy power of God's love, for paw-holding, church-going, and possibly raising a family of kittens. No fanatics or unemployed toms, please.

WHY YOU WANT TO GET TO KNOW ME: I'm humble, kind, and gentle. I would support my tom without question, because I know my love for him makes us both stronger. Of course, if you think I'm going to sit idly by while you try to sacrifice one of our sons because the voices in your head are telling you to, we're definitely on different pages of the Bible.

MY IDEAL DATE INCLUDES: First, we'd go to Mass, to cleanse our hearts of sin and wash away lustful thoughts. Afterwards, you would escort me home, and if we felt it wasn't too improper, we would sit outside my house for a little while, not touching or talking but just appreciating the beauty of the moment. Repeat 12 times, then we'd get married, have kittens, and grow old together.

MY MOTTO: Cats must be God's favorite creatures—Jesus had two lives, but we have nine!

SEX
KITTENS
112

PERSONALS

WHISKER ME AWAY

WHAT I'M LOOKING FOR: Smart and witty PAT with a sophisticated bent and a romantic bone in his body. Must like games, flirting, riddles. Can you do a Saturday *New York Times* puzzle in ink? Let's talk, shall we?

WHY YOU WANT TO GET TO KNOW ME: I think the brain is an erogenous zone, and the path to my heart is definitely through my mind—a clever turn of phrase will inspire me to, ahem, "present" more quickly than a tired old display of testosterone.

WHAT'S IN MY BEDROOM: Reading light, Black Warrior pencils (No. 2), highlighters, the concise edition of the *OED*, and trophies I've won at *Scrabble* competitions. Also, I have a taste for lacy underwear, so don't think it's all about wordplay—foreplay's important, too.

A SECRET MOST OTHERS DON'T KNOW ABOUT ME: I have a crush on Will Shortz, though I dearly miss the sure hand of Eugene T. Maleska.

MY MOTTO: What's a two-letter synonym for "stimulating"? M-E!

Meow!

SEX
KITTENS
113

Minimalist Seeks Mate

From: queen3478221
Sent: Sunday, July 17, 2005 10:35 AM
To: CAT
Subject: RE: Minimalist Seeks Mate

WHAT I'M LOOKING FOR: CAQ seeks well-groomed CAT with an aversion to clutter. Doesn't track litter or scatter food, doesn't bring home half-eaten animals like a common yard-cat.

WHY YOU WANT TO GET TO KNOW ME: I like things simple, whether it's a perfectly timed grooming session or a single-flavor cat food (dry, of course, and pre-measured). Also, I'm knowledgeable in the art of Feng Shui.

WHAT I'M READING: A biography of Mies van der Rohe, the most recent catalog for The Container Store, *Real Simple* magazine.

MY IDEAL DATE INCLUDES: You would help me move all the furniture around, and then we would stare at the carpet looking for any frayed fibers that need to be clipped.

I'M MOST NEUROTIC ABOUT: Bold patterns and stripes.

MY MOTTO: God is in the lack of details.

Classy Homemaker Seeks Long-Term Houseguest

WHAT I'M LOOKING FOR: CWQ wants to meet a sophisticated PA/WT who can appreciate the fine art of home entertaining. You bring the witty banter and good table manners, and I'll bring the hospitality—and possibly dessert....

WHY YOU WANT TO GET TO KNOW ME: I'm a perfectionist who won't rest until everything is just right. I have impeccable taste. I'm a hard worker. I always make sure I have the best dish for any get together.

WHAT I'M READING: Anything related to Martha Stewart. Magazines: *Nest*, *Real Simple*, and of course, *Architectural Digest*.

MY IDEAL DATE INCLUDES: I would love to make my special tom a five course meal unlike anything he's ever tasted, designed to seduce the senses from first bite to last, in my beautifully decorated dining room.

MY MOTTO: It's not perfect until it's perfect.

Hottie!

SEX KITTENS 115

Country Queen Seeks Move to the City

WHAT I'M LOOKING FOR: CAQ iso PA/WT who lives in the city and is willing to take a country bumpkin back with him. Residents of Chicago and San Francisco a plus.

WHY YOU WANT TO GET TO KNOW ME: I'm sick of living in this barn with a bunch of hicks! I really think I was switched at birth...I know I am way more sophisticated than anyone around here and I am ready for the urban life.

WHAT'S IN MY BEDROOM: My collection of hats, a reprint of Monet's *Water Lilies*, and a hideous needlepoint my person made me that I'll be happy to get rid of.

BEST/WORST/BIGGEST LIE I EVER TOLD: "I'd love some more grits."

MY MOTTO: I'm ready to move on up.

SEX KITTENS 116

Don't Want To Be Hurt Again

What I'm Looking For: CAQ wants to meet CAT, someone I can trust, who won't lie, cheat on me, or raise a paw. I just got out of an abusive relationship and I'm still feeling pretty vulnerable.

Why You Want To Get To Know Me: I can be a devoted, considerate partner if you give me a reason. I like quiet romantic evenings alone with you, or going hunting as a pair.

What I'm Reading/Watching: Toms Who Run with the Pack, and the Queens Who Love Them. On TV: *Dr. Phil, Oprah, Starting Over.*

Best/Worst/Biggest Lie I Ever Told:
I hated the pet bird we got last year, so one day I ate it, then carefully cleaned up the mess and pretended it got out and flew away.

My Motto:
I am responsible for my own happiness.

Meow!

SEX
KITTENS
117

Don't Let Me Do It!

From: queen999
Sent: Monday, July 18, 2005 @ 3:13 PM
To: CAT
Subject: RE: Don't Let Me Do It!

WHAT I'M LOOKING FOR: CWQ looking to meet CAT who can talk me down from this ledge.

WHY YOU WANT TO GET TO KNOW ME: I've been pretty depressed lately and have already gone through six of my lives (I know how to not land on my feet). I'm ready for a sensitive tom who can show me why life is worth living.

MY IDEAL DATE INCLUDES: You bring me flowers and then we eat them.

MY FAVORITE PHYSICAL ACTIVITIES: I love to climb: poles, trees, houses, and sometimes people if I dislike them enough or they're holding out on me with food.

MY MOTTO: Thank goodness for nine lives.

SEX KITTENS 118

PERSONALS

DESPERATE HOUSEPETS DATING SERVICE

¿TU QUIERES MI AMIGO?

WHAT I'M LOOKING FOR: Petite but powerful CWQ wants a P/C A/W tom who lives in the southwest region of U.S. Not looking for romance just yet—just a partner in crime. Come be the Clyde to my Bonnie.

WHY YOU WANT TO GET TO KNOW ME: Don't underestimate the power of looking so dainty. I can get almost anything I want by looking cute and mewing in a high-pitched voice. And if that doesn't work, I'm an expert at pick-pocketing.

WHAT I'M WATCHING: Any telenovela starring Mauricio Islas. *The Honeymoon Killers, Jackie Brown.*

I'M MOST NEUROTIC ABOUT: Getting stuck in the wrong backyard patrolled by a big, unfriendly dog.

MY MOTTO: Life is like a piñata; you just have to keep swinging away and eventually you'll be rewarded.

SEX
KITTENS
119

Tired of Singing the Blues

WHAT I'M LOOKING FOR: CWQ iso CWT. Need to hear from a fun-loving tom who'll bring some happy melodies into my life. I've spent too many years living out the blues, and I'm ready to spice up the night with a jazzier sound.

WHY YOU WANT TO GET TO KNOW ME: I've got a voice like Billie Holiday, and I can make my trumpet purr.

MY IDEAL DATE INCLUDES: You pick me up early for a light dinner, and then we seek out a good location—ideally in a hard-to-reach area that's still within listening distance of humans—where we spend the next several hours scatting and riffing on the exotic sounds of yowling. As dawn approaches, you take me home and we sleep like stones, content and exhausted.

MY DREAM VACATION: New Orleans, where we can visit Preservation Hall and eat *beignets*.

MY MOTTO: We can make beautiful music together.

SEX KITTENS 120

SEXY FELINE MACHINE!

Ready to Confess My Dirtiest Secrets

From: queen1056
Sent: Wednesday, July 6, 2005 @ 6:03 PM
To: CAT
Subject: RE: Ready to Confess My Dirtiest Secrets

WHAT I'M LOOKING FOR: CAQ wants a proper, upright CAT, preferably with a Catholic background, for a little sensual "confessional booth" play. You: be quiet, mature, with a more libido—understand that sex is more than just wild rutting in the alley (although we can do that, too, as long as I can "confess" it later!).

WHY YOU WANT TO GET TO KNOW ME: I'm a normal-seeming feline with a respectable family, but I have a secret streak of kink running through me that I only share with my fellow playmates. Love role-playing, toys, light bondage, and bible-humping.

WHAT I'M READING/WATCHING: Currently reading the diary of Anais Nin, also enjoy the *Sleeping Beauty* books of A.N. Rocquelaure. I love old re-runs of *The Red Shoe Diaries*, and anything on Cinemax after midnight.

BEST/WORST/BIGGEST LIE I EVER TOLD: I once pretended I knocked over a lamp, when really the dog did it, just for some QT with the monsignor.

MY MOTTO: How many Hail Marys for carnal relations with a dog!?

SEX
KITTENS
121

Empress of Living Room
Needs New Subject to Rule

WHAT I'M LOOKING FOR: PAQ seeks loyal PAT peasant to worship me from afar. You stay on the floor, or in the hallway, while I hold court on the sofa. You watch me eat and then feast on my scraps as I'm washing my whiskers. You find your own litter box. If any part of the house smells like you, then you'll be clapped in irons and tossed into the cellar with the dog.

WHY YOU WANT TO GET TO KNOW ME: I'm a kind and generous ruler who will always choose to grant mercy if I feel that it's deserved (which it almost always isn't).

WHAT'S IN MY BEDROOM: I sleep in a custom-built bed, lined in warm flannel and filled with a downy mattress. My bed chamber also has two massive, specially designed machines, one to provide pleasing white noise to mask the inane chatter of the humans, and one to provide warmth and a gentle vibration when I desire it. As a show of respect, the humans here fill plastic baskets with items of clothing to put in the machines, so that they will run continuously.

I'M MOST NEUROTIC ABOUT: My owners not being able to find my pedigree certificate in time for a show.

MY MOTTO: If it's good enough for you, it's probably not good enough for me.

SEX
KITTENS
122

Beach Bunny Needs Surf Stud

What I'm Looking For: CWQ needs a sporty, well-built, CAT who considers the beach his second home. You should be able to fish and enjoy playing with/eating live crabs.

Why You Want To Get To Know Me: I know all the best spots in the area: where to get the most sun, where to catch the fattest mice, which houses provide the best scraps, and what beaches have the fewest humans. I always have a nice tan, but I don't think looks matter as much as my outlook on life, which is very laid-back and cool.

My Dream Vacation: To a lot of cats, I'm probably living their dream vacation, but to be honest I'd love to visit a forest some day. I want to know what it feels like to be rub my gums on the rough bark. I'd also love to catch a squirrel.

Best/Worst/Biggest Lie I Ever Told: When I was still a kitten, I told my friend that I could swim, and when he called me a liar I jumped into the surf to prove him wrong. A lifeguard had to rescue me. It was very embarrassing.

My Motto: I'm the catch of the day, every day.

SEX
KITTENS
123

I'm Tired of Being Admired

WHAT I'M LOOKING FOR:
A common tom who doesn't have any attitude or delusions of grandeur, who can appreciate me as a cat first, a queen second, and a registered Balinese with a pedigree a distant third.

WHY YOU WANT TO GET TO KNOW ME: Though I'm worshipped as a goddess in some parts of the world, I'm really very down-to-earth, if you'll give me a chance. I'm also a celebrated master of Balinese gamelan music.

MY IDEAL DATE INCLUDES: Climbing into an alley dumpster and scavenging for food. Maybe picking a fight with some stray tabbies.

I'M MOST NEUROTIC ABOUT: Q-Tips.

MY MOTTO: Love *me*, not my pedigree.

SEX KITTENS 124

Meow!

PERSONALS

DESPERATE HOUSEPETS DATING SERVICE

LEO SEEKS LOVE MATCH

WHAT I'M LOOKING FOR:
PAQ needs PAT who
is a Cancer, Aries,
Sagittarius, or Gemini
ONLY. I believe in the
stars and my psychic
told me those are my
only matches.

**WHY YOU WANT TO GET TO
KNOW ME:** I'm a lion-lady
Leo who roars her way
through life—that
includes the bedroom.
My kisses are wild and
uninhibited, I enjoy biting
and clawing and I expect
applause for my perform-
ance. Plus, when I went
to a paw reader she
told me I would live
a long life.

WHAT'S IN MY BEDROOM: Stacks of the horoscope section from the
newspaper, Susan Miller's *The Year Ahead*, deck of tarot cards, a crystal
ball, a phone bill from my calls to 1-800-PSYCHIC.

BEST/WORST/BIGGEST LIE I EVER TOLD: I once told a Libra that I was a
Pisces so he would date me. Naturally, our relationship was disastrous.

MY MOTTO: Love is in the stars.

SEX
KITTENS
125

Bird Watcher Wants to Watch You

WHAT I'M LOOKING FOR: Young, adventurous queen seeks PWT who shares my love of bird-watching (and eating) and tree-climbing. Must be able to scale tall trees and get down again without mewing for help. Knowledge of bird-calls a plus.

WHY YOU WANT TO GET TO KNOW ME: I began bird-watching as a kitten, and was soon honing my climbing skills on large houseplants and, eventually, on the Christmas tree. I'm now an outdoor kitty who can climb any tree and catch a little feathered snack whenever I want. I'm looking for a partner to double my intake.

WHAT'S IN MY BEDROOM: Binoculars, my feather collection (I keep one from each bird that I catch), a copy of *Peterson's Field Guide to the Birds of North America*.

WHAT I'M LISTENING TO: My favorite piece of music is Respighi's *Pines of Rome*, but I also enjoy listening to my CD of bird-calls.

I'M MOST NEUROTIC ABOUT: Not landing on my feet.

MY MOTTO: Life is best lived in the treetops.

SEX KITTENS 126

Help Me Free Dino

From: queen1917
Sent: Sunday, May 1, 2005 @ 8:00 AM
To: C/PA/WT
Subject: RE: Help Me Free Dino

WHAT I'M LOOKING FOR: CAQ seeks any tom who can help me rescue Dino from behind the iron curtain. He cries out to me that he can't breathe, but I'm not strong enough to lift him.

WHY YOU WANT TO GET TO KNOW ME: As you can see, I've finally learned to unlock the door. Working as a team, we can free Dino from his misery. Once this is accomplished, we can adopt him as our child. He's had such a hard life, I can't wait to be a loving mother to him.

WHAT I'M READING/LISTENING TO/WATCHING: Old *Flintstones* reruns that show Dino as a freewheeling pet.

A SECRET MOST OTHERS DON'T KNOW ABOUT ME: Closed doors make me crazy.

MY MOTTO: Hold on for one more day, little buddy!

SEX KITTENS 127

Not Picky

WHAT I'M LOOKING FOR: CAQ seeks regular P/CAT for companionship in a largely rule-free household. Must be self-sufficient and independent, especially regarding human contact. We'll keep each other company—and no human can scratch your haunches like I can.

WHY YOU WANT TO GET TO KNOW ME: I live in a do-it-yourself household, so pampered pets or those used to lots of people interaction may find it a shock; the last tom I was seeing couldn't adjust to the solitude and had to leave. That's why I only want to meet other cats who don't mind doing without clean kitty litter and the occasional lap. I can also make a mean smoked-salmon omelet.

WHAT'S IN MY BEDROOM: Scraps of old food, hairballs, and an ammonia odor that could peel paint.

MY DREAM VACATION: Camping in the mountains where we catch our own food and create our own shelter.

MY MOTTO: Latch-key kitties make better lovers...and breakfast.

Call Tonight!

SEX KITTENS 128

Club Kitten Seeks Raver

What I'm Looking For:
Sexy, energetic kitty into techno, jungle, and trance music seeks a spunky tom who can keep up with me on the dance floor.

Why You Want To Get To Know Me: I'm a tiger on the dance floor, but my stamina is 100% natural—no catnip! I'm very popular on the rave scene and can take you beyond the velvet ropes of all the most exclusive under-ground clubs.

My Ideal Date Includes: We meet for pizza at around 10:00 and hit the clubs by midnight. Then we dance until dawn and you walk me home as the sun rises.

I'm Most Neurotic About: My catty flirtatiousness failing to work on a bouncer.

My Motto: "You make me feel like dancin'."

SEX
KITTENS
129

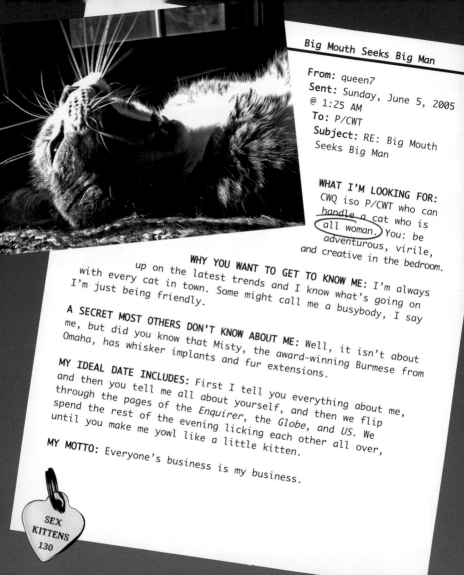

Big Mouth Seeks Big Man

From: queen7
Sent: Sunday, June 5, 2005 @ 1:25 AM
To: P/CWT
Subject: RE: Big Mouth Seeks Big Man

WHAT I'M LOOKING FOR: CWQ iso P/CWT who can handle a cat who is all woman. You: be adventurous, virile, and creative in the bedroom.

WHY YOU WANT TO GET TO KNOW ME: I'm always up on the latest trends and I know what's going on with every cat in town. Some might call me a busybody, I say I'm just being friendly.

A SECRET MOST OTHERS DON'T KNOW ABOUT ME: Well, it isn't about me, but did you know that Misty, the award-winning Burmese from Omaha, has whisker implants and fur extensions.

MY IDEAL DATE INCLUDES: First I tell you everything about me, and then you tell me all about yourself, and then we flip through the pages of the *Enquirer*, the *Globe*, and *US*. We spend the rest of the evening licking each other all over, until you make me yowl like a little kitten.

MY MOTTO: Everyone's business is my business.

SEX KITTENS
130

PERSONALS

FIND ME BEFORE I LOSE MY FRESHNESS

WHAT I'M LOOKING FOR: PWQ iso PAT. I'm saving myself for the perfect tom—is that you? I need a cat who is sensitive, kind, generous, and thoughtful. Please, no rough-and-tumble types, and no one night stands.

WHY YOU WANT TO GET TO KNOW ME: I'm pure as can be and I'm holding out on sex until I meet the right tom. I'm clean and sweet and I want to experience the miracle of intimacy before I'm too old.

WHAT'S IN MY BEDROOM: Lots of ruffles, ribbons, and lace. Oh, and everything is in pink.

I'M MOST NEUROTIC ABOUT: My refrigerator time. (Thirty minutes every day keeps me fresh and pure.) Getting old and wrinkly before I find the right tom.

THE BEST/WORST/BIGGEST LIE I EVER TOLD: I told my ex I couldn't sleep with him because I was waiting until marriage. Really, he just smelled bad.

MY MOTTO: I'm 100% organic with no preservatives.

SEX
KITTENS
131

Come Try Me Out

WHAT I'M LOOKING FOR: An adventurous P/CAT who likes to experiment in the bedroom. Toms who have their own stash of toys are more than welcome. Anyone who can bend back as far as I can.

WHY YOU WANT TO GET TO KNOW ME: My owners just bought me this brand-new, state-of-the-art sex apparatus. I'm not sure why, but I don't really care. I already know it works great solo and I can't wait to try out with a partner. It assists with multiple, unique positions and makes things much more interesting.

WHAT'S IN MY BEDROOM: See picture above. I also have a hookah and some Marvin Gaye records.

MY DREAM VACATION: The store where this thing came from.

MY MOTTO: If it feels good, do it.

SEX KITTENS 132

SEXY FELINE MACHINE!

Do I Look Fat to You?

From: queen10
Sent: Saturday, July 9, 2005 @ 6:30 PM
To: PAT
Subject: RE: Do I Look Fat to You?

WHAT I'M LOOKING FOR: A tom who will be honest with me. Someone who understands my hang-ups and loves me anyway. Slightly neurotic a plus.

WHY YOU WANT TO GET TO KNOW ME: Though I'm self-conscious about my looks (I was a chubster when I was a kitten and I've been on every diet in the book), I'm very sensitive and always willing to help. I even work as a counselor at Fat Cats Anonymous.

WHAT'S IN MY BEDROOM: A mirror, a scale, and a case of Walkers Shortbread—temptation keeps me strong!

A SECRET MOST OTHERS DON'T KNOW ABOUT ME: I used to work as a butt-double for Kirstie Alley.

BEST/WORST/BIGGEST LIE I EVER TOLD: Of course I can eat just one!

MY MOTTO: Jenny Craig deserves the Congressional Medal of Honor.

SEX KITTENS 133

Attack of the 50-Ft. Housecat

WHAT I'M LOOKING FOR: Preternaturally enormous CWT with a heart of gold (or at least sterling silver!); must weigh at least 6,000 lbs. You are a freak of nature or lab-created mutant searching for a queen who knows what it is like to live as a giant in the world. No smokers or alcoholics, please—I live in the forests of Montana, where tobacco and booze are both hard to come by and fire is the enemy.

WHY YOU WANT TO GET TO KNOW ME: Well, how many other 50-foot-tall female members of Felis silvestris catus do you know of? Seriously, if our statures are compatible, we should meet; I'm a compassionate, even-tempered, and very horny CWQ with a philosophical outlook on life. How else to survive little to no feline companionship and having to eat moose, deer, and other woodland creatures?

WHAT'S IN MY BEDROOM: My bedroom is an enormous moss-lined clearing in the woods near Bozeman, so the sky is my blanket and the earth is my bed.

A SECRET MOST OTHERS DON'T KNOW ABOUT ME: I carry on a one-feline protest against "big lumber" by using their field offices as my litter box.

MY MOTTO: Milk! Milk! I'd trade my left eye for a swimming pool full of milk.

SEX KITTENS 134

Easter Kitty Seeks Help

What I'm Looking For: Loopy CWQ really needs a strong CAT to guide me through life and love. I'm a lovely creature, really, but I do need some help sorting out the voices in my head.

Why You Want To Get To Know Me: I suffer from occasional delusional behavior, but don't let that scare you. It's just that sometimes I think I'm a hen. And sometimes the Easter Bunny. But if I take my medication then I'm fine. I swear I'm fine. I'm not crazy. Really.

My Ideal Date Includes: We'd cluck around the pen for a while and peck at each other. Wait, no, shut up, I'm a cat, dammit! No, I'm a giant pink rabbit! No, I'm a cat! Hang on a minute here....

A Secret Most Others Don't Know About Me: My mother was a jackalope.

I'm Most Neurotic About: Getting my feathers dirty.

My Motto: Did I mention I'm not crazy?

SEX KITTENS 135

Great-Great-Great Granny Ready for Round 9

WHAT I'M LOOKING FOR: CWQ, well into her 9th life, seeks gentle CW/A tom to spend the golden years with. Should be an experienced mouser who enjoys providing for his queen. No whippersnappers; must be 12 years old or older, and preferably have all (or at least most) of your teeth.

WHY YOU WANT TO GET TO KNOW ME: I'm a feisty grandma with a comfy home. Been an empty-nester (both feline and human) for six years now and loving it—don't want/need any more kittens or children. Not interested in travel or the stray life, either—if you've got a wanderin' spirit, keep on going, traveler.

WHAT'S IN MY BEDROOM: Crocheted cat bed with a picture of a goose on it, and an electric blanket.

MY IDEAL DATE INCLUDES: Going out for the early-bird special then coming home for a nice evening of Matlock and Maalox.

MY MOTTO: Life begins at fifteen!

SEX
KITTENS
136

PERSONALS

HELLO? IS ANYBODY OUT THERE?

WHAT I'M LOOKING FOR: Serious, intense PWQ seeks artistic P/C A/WT who's not afraid to feel. Poets and writers welcome; toms in gray flannel suits need not apply.

WHY YOU WANT TO GET TO KNOW ME: I'm a little mysterious, a bit of a riddle in feline form. I can be sexy and sultry one minute, introspective the next. I love to paint, chase shadows, and stare at the rain. I'm pretty self-absorbed, but not selfish. I give great tail-root scratches.

WHAT I'M READING: My favorite books are *Songs of Innocence* and *Songs of Experience* by William Blake.

BEST/WORST/BIGGEST LIE I EVER TOLD: When I was younger, before I had discovered myself, I once pretended to be an airhead to get a tom to like me.

MY MOTTO: "Tyger! Tyger! burning bright/In the forest of the night/What immortal hand or eye/Could frame thy fearful symmetry?"

SEX
KITTENS
137

See Anything You Like?

WHAT I'M LOOKING FOR: Sexy CAQ needs AT, breed not important, for sensual adventures. It would be nice if you had more on your mind than just sex, but I'll settle for physically gifted and single-minded. Anyway, must be uninhibited and eager to try new things. Limber toms preferred.

WHY YOU WANT TO GET TO KNOW ME: I'm proud of my body and I want to share it with an appreciative cat. And, who knows? This could be the start of a beautiful relationship!

WHAT'S IN MY BEDROOM: Incense, massage oils, a mirror on the ceiling. My collection of special "adult kitty" videos I like to watch to put me and my partners in the mood.

A SECRET MOST OTHER DON'T KNOW ABOUT ME: I have a dander problem.

MY MOTTO: A kiss on the lips is quite continental, but a cunning linguist is a girl's best friend.

Meow!

SEX
KITTENS
138

Let's Take Things Slowly (Or Not At All)

From: queen269
Sent: Friday, April 29, 2005 @ 1:25 AM
To: CA/WT
Subject: RE: Let's Take Things Slowly (Or Not At All)

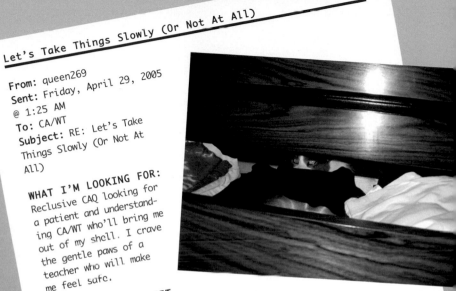

WHAT I'M LOOKING FOR: Reclusive CAQ looking for a patient and understanding CA/WT who'll bring me out of my shell. I crave the gentle paws of a teacher who will make me feel safe.

WHY YOU WANT TO GET TO KNOW ME: I'm very intelligent and might be a lot of fun to be around, but if so, only in one-on-one encounters. Not big on new people, cats, places, foods, furniture, sounds, or smells. You must be willing to take things slow at first, and stay indoors at all times.

MY IDEAL DATE INCLUDES: I think a lot of cats rush into things too quickly these days. I'd prefer to start slow—maybe a postcard or a short email message? Then we could take it from there, and if we really hit it off, meet face-to-face by our third or fourth date.

A SECRET MOST OTHERS DON'T KNOW ABOUT ME: There's no way I'm sharing my secrets in a personal ad.

MY MOTTO: Cedar-lined drawers stink.

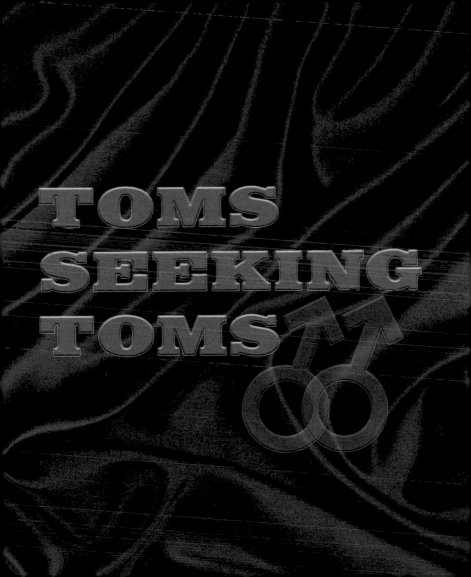

Starving Artist Needs Patron

From: tom563
Sent: Tuesday, July 19, 2005 @ 12:03 PM
To: CWT
Subject: RE: Starving Artist Needs Patron

WHAT I'M LOOKING FOR: I'm a young, up-and-coming avant-garde artist looking for emotional and financial support. You: be a successful, sophisticated CWT who recognizes talent and understands that me are high maintenance and need to be pampered. Connections in the art world a plus. Older toms (15 and up) preferred.

WHY YOU WANT TO GET TO KNOW ME: I'm a passionate, complicated kitty with a flair for the dramatic. I can be moody and ferociously jealous, but when I have a moment of calm I can be adorable. I also make great arm-candy at gallery openings.

WHAT'S IN MY BEDROOM: Several *assemblage* sculptures in progress. A pile of found objects. A couple of my friends are staying over right now, too, just until they find some homes of their own.

MY IDEAL DATE INCLUDES: A trip to Venice for the *Biennale* followed by two weeks in Capri.

MY MOTTO: Truth is beauty, and beauty is financial security.

ALOHA, KITTY!

WHAT I'M LOOKING FOR: Laid back but playful CAT iso CWT for lazy but passionate afternoons of exploration and napping on the beautiful island of Maui. Enthusiastic nipheads only, please.

WHY YOU WANT TO GET TO KNOW ME: I have a 30-acre ranch on Maui, where I grow some of the best catnip you'll ever sample, and I'd love to share it with the right cat. Napping is probably my top priority, followed closely by "nipping."

MY IDEAL DATE INCLUDES: We each put a pinch of nip between our cheek and gums, blend up a couple of mai tais, and spend the afternoon lolling around on the beach or by my pool.

WHAT I'M READING/WATCHING: I just finished Jimmy Buffett's *Tales from Margaritaville* and am starting *Corelli's Mandolin*. Some of my favorite DVDs are *Magnum P.I.: The Complete Series*, *Breakfast at Tiffany's*, and *Mosquito Coast*.

MY MOTTO: I love the island life.

Hunky Stud!

SEX KITTENS 143

Wizard of Loneliness Seeks Magician of Love

WHAT I'M LOOKING FOR: I'm a PWT who got out of a long-term relationship six months ago, and I'm ready to get back into the dating scene. You are a sensitive, affectionate tom, breed doesn't matter, who enjoys the finer things in life: lounging with a good book, taking drives in the country, destroying upholstered furniture, etc.

WHY YOU WANT TO GET TO KNOW ME: I'm a soulful, handsome (so I'm told) cat with lots of love to give. I'm also a great cook and speak several languages. Plus I have a huge, overstuffed sectional sofa in my house, which my person gave up on long ago. It's covered in that silky, loopy fabric—the crème de la crème of scratchin' upholstery.

MY IDEAL DATE INCLUDES: A romantic dinner for two at home: field mouse *en croûte* with a salad of tender wheat grass, followed by liver mousse topped with crème fraiche.

WHAT I'M READING/LISTENING TO/WATCHING: I admit I'm a Food Network addict, but I also love to watch old movies. William Powell is one of my favorite actors. I love him in the *Thin Man* films and *My Man Godfrey*.

MY MOTTO: Why scratch alone?

SEX KITTENS 144

Crafty Cat Will Decorate Your Life with Love

From: tom10001
Sent: Monday, July 18, 2005 @ 4:13 PM
To: CA/WT
Subject: RE: Crafty Cat Will Decorate Your Life with Love

WHAT I'M LOOKING FOR: CAT wants CA/WT with a talent for crafts and a belief that life's better when you add felt and pipe cleaners! You should know the basics: fabric painting, scrapbooking, hot glue-gunning. Sex is important, but so is the ability to make your own gift soap.

WHY YOU WANT TO GET TO KNOW ME: I've got a limitless imagination. I love to make things and give them to friends, whether it's a set of crocheted booties for those cold winter nights or a coffee mug with a mouse painted on it. But I have a kinky side, too! I love to wear hand-stamped leather outfits, I can tie knots that even Boy Scouts don't know, and I can do things with my gluestick that would make your mother blush.

WHAT I'M READING/WATCHING: On TV: Christopher Lowell's *Wall-to-Wall*, anything on the Do-It-Yourself Channel, *Brini Maxwell* Season 1 DVD. Favorite book: *Seven Layers of Design* by Christopher Lowell.

A SECRET MOST OTHERS DON'T KNOW ABOUT ME: I once tried to Bedazzle my tail and had to be taken to the vet to have rhinestones removed. Handy tip: if it looks like a stapler, back away.

MY MOTTO: Everything looks better decoupaged.

SEX KITTENS 145

Daddy Lion Seeks Cub to Train

WHAT I'M LOOKING FOR: Young, inexperienced PWT for this CAT to turn into a fully-grown tomcat. You: be polite, eager to please, attitude-free. Willing to submit to a big daddy type who knows how he wants his boy to behave. Please be sane.

WHY YOU WANT TO GET TO KNOW ME: Because I'm big, and it's all either muscle or hair. I have a tough, butt-kicking exterior, but if you're one of the lucky few who can get past the outer shell, you'll discover I can be as meek as a week-old kitten without her momma.

MY IDEAL DATE INCLUDES: You'll show up on time or be severely punished. I'll hold you down and roughly clean your ears and neck, and then teach you a thing or two about how to fight like a tom and not a little kitty.

A SECRET MOST OTHERS DON'T KNOW ABOUT ME IS: I was declawed as a child, so I wear falsies.

MY MOTTO: I'm the king of the forest, baby.

Hunky Stud!

Ready for My Love Bath

What I'm Looking For: I'm a PAT iso same. Should enjoy sensual activities like long and slow brushing, consensual licking, quality time with humans who will scratch behind the ears, and bubble baths. Must be good conversationalist. Great hygiene and strong level of self-esteem are a must. Be disease free, not neurotic, not too needy, absolutely not competitive.

Why You Want To Get To Know Me:
Because I'm a soft and cuddly love tiger, that's why!
I want to be able to snuggle up next to you and make you feel like you're home again.

What I'm Watching: I have all of the original British *Queer as Folk* series on DVD and love to watch them, although the American version is good, too. Also love to watch any reality show that involves nannies or housekeepers.

I'm Most Neurotic About: The possibility that some day the humans might want to get a dog—or worse, a baby.

My Motto: It takes a village to prevent mats in your fur.

SEX
KITTENS
147

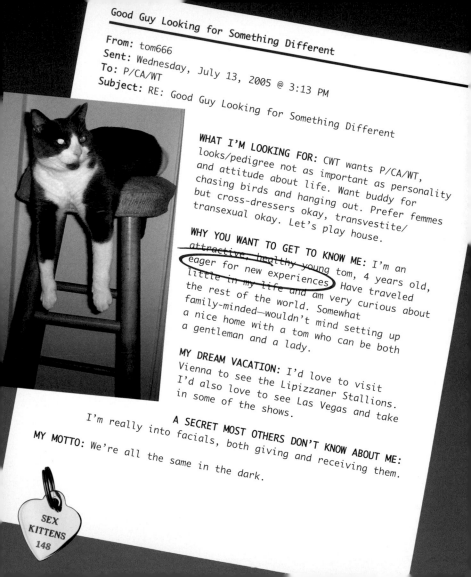

Good Guy Looking for Something Different

From: tom666
Sent: Wednesday, July 13, 2005 @ 3:13 PM
To: P/CA/WT
Subject: RE: Good Guy Looking for Something Different

WHAT I'M LOOKING FOR: CWT wants P/CA/WT, looks/pedigree not as important as personality and attitude about life. Want buddy for chasing birds and hanging out. Prefer femmes but cross-dressers okay, transvestite/transexual okay. Let's play house.

WHY YOU WANT TO GET TO KNOW ME: I'm an attractive, healthy young tom, 4 years old, eager for new experiences. Have traveled little in my life and am very curious about the rest of the world. Somewhat family-minded—wouldn't mind setting up a nice home with a tom who can be both a gentleman and a lady.

MY DREAM VACATION: I'd love to visit Vienna to see the Lipizzaner Stallions. I'd also love to see Las Vegas and take in some of the shows.

A SECRET MOST OTHERS DON'T KNOW ABOUT ME: I'm really into facials, both giving and receiving them.

MY MOTTO: We're all the same in the dark.

PERSONALS

ENERGIZER BUNNY SEEKS FRESH BATTERIES

WHAT I'M LOOKING FOR: CAT iso another CAT who's up for some old-fashioned wrasslin'. Also, I love rubbing my cheeks against rough surfaces. I'm looking for good clean fun, but am not averse to a little catnip now and then. No meth addicts, please.

WHY YOU WANT TO GET TO KNOW ME: I'm young and full o' beans, not one of those lazy kitties who can't even be bothered to bat at

a cat-dancer. I mean, really, how could anyone resist the cat-dancer!?

MY IDEAL DATE INCLUDES: We'd do a few laps around the room, then try jumping to the top of the bookcase. Next, we'd see who can catch the housefly first. Whoever succeeds gets a full-body scratch from the loser, with extra attention given to the small of the back. If we have any energy left, we can rub our gums against the doorjamb.

A SECRET MOST OTHERS DON'T KNOW ABOUT ME: I have a secret hideout on the top shelf of my person's closet, behind the winter coats. He has no idea I can get up there.

MY MOTTO: Life Is best lived at top speed.

Call Tonight!

SEX KITTENS 149

Risk-Taker Seeks Stunt Coordinator

From: tom444
Sent: Friday, July 15, 2005 @ 4:43 PM
To: CA/WT
Subject: RE: Risk-Taker Seeks Stunt Coordinator

WHAT I'M LOOKING FOR:
A masculine tom who won't nag me about my feel-good approach to life. I'm a CAT; you: be a CA/WT who knows that it's not about the quantity of lives you live, but the quality.

WHY YOU WANT TO GET TO KNOW ME: I'm a pretty regular tom who doesn't go for anything too fancy or frilly, but I'm always up for a good time. I once stowed away under the hood of a car and took a surprise trip to the supermarket parking lot, which was awesome. If that kind of adventure sounds fun to you, let me know and we'll trade ideas.

WHAT I'M WATCHING: *Most Extreme Challenge*, *Jackass*, hockey games (for the fights), and the Iditarod (boy are dogs dumb!).

I'M MOST NEUROTIC ABOUT: One day finding myself with the same lifestyle as those fat, lazy breeders who do nothing their whole lives but sleep and mate.

MY MOTTO: If god didn't want me to ride the spin cycle, he would have made the washing machine cat-proof.

Basically Straight—Just Curious Is All

WHAT I'M LOOKING FOR: I'm a young-ish CAT between girl-friends, curious about sex with other toms. I'm looking for a straight-acting P/C A/W T with experience. Must have own place where we can meet. Can't make any promises, but let's get together, have some beers, and see what happens from there.

WHY YOU WANT TO GET TO KNOW ME: I'm good-looking, intelligent, discreet. Not into stalking or getting too serious or anything like that. I don't like playing games—I want to keep it nice, friendly, and fair—I'll show you mine if you show me yours.

WHAT'S IN MY BEDROOM: A stack of old *Vanity Fair* issues, the current *GQ*, a medium-sized collection of skin creams and lotions. I take good care of myself—I think that's important for a single cat.

I'M MOST NEUROTIC ABOUT: My owners catching me "experimenting" and getting the wrong idea.

MY MOTTO: Curiosity got the cat laid.

SEX KITTENS 151

Let's Make Magic Together

WHAT I'M LOOKING FOR: Spiritually adventurous PAT iso open, courageous CWT to assist me with my rituals as well as in my bedroom. Be a deep thinker. Looks not important, but no femmes. Must have an appreciation of nature, love to read, and be interested in the dark and awesome power of candlemagic. No Wiccans!

WHY YOU WANT TO GET TO KNOW ME: Because I can give you the kind of power you only dreamed of, power over your friends and enemies, over humans, over the stars—or at least power over me, but only if we agree on a safe word first.

MY IDEAL DATE INCLUDES: Uttering dark enchantments. We'd circle the small altar I sometimes set up in the basement when my owners are at work. Primarily we'll be cursing my owners, but after that, if you want to get a curse or two in there, feel free. I used to do a lot of hot wax play, but it's almost impossible to get wax out of fur.

BEST/WORST/BIGGEST LIE I EVER TOLD: I've "happily" posed for the family Christmas card two years running. The fools! The pathetic fools!

MY MOTTO: Feed me wet food, or else!

SEX KITTENS 152

Is There Life After Three (Years in Prison)?

What I'm Looking For: Hardcore CWT wants P/CA/WT for friendship/relationship/messing around. You be any age between 1 and dead, as long as you're strong and confident. Burly toms with similar pasts preferred. Into group scenes, too, so get in touch if you're getting a party started.

Why You Want To Get To Know Me: I may look small, but I'm a scrappy fighter who's survived every curve-ball that life's thrown at me so far. Sure, I've lost most of my tail. Sure, I got a little bit of a limp on my hind leg. Sure, I've made mistakes, but who hasn't? You gonna brag that you're perfect? I can take care of that real quick.

A Secret Most Others Don't Know About Me: I know how to give tattoos using an old cassette player, a sewing needle, and a ballpoint pen.

I'm Most Neurotic About: Sirens, flashing lights, thick black rubber gloves, and any sort of cat carrier.

My Motto: A tossed salad ain't so bad if you use the right dressing.

SEX KITTENS 153

I Look Better From Behind!

From: tom10007
Sent: Thursday, July 7, 2005 @ 7:03 PM
To: CA/WT
Subject: RE: I Look Better From Behind!

WHAT I'M LOOKING FOR: CAT needs sleazy back-alley sex with a hot, hung CA/WT. You: be aggressive, verbal, very butch, a little rough. Prefer pound toms and strays over pampered housecats like myself.

WHY YOU WANT TO GET TO KNOW ME: I'm a house-bound tom with a good home and too much food (yawn!), and I need to be taught a lesson. I'm a real yowler.

MY IDEAL DATE INCLUDES: Date? If you wanna call it that, okay, sure. Basically what I need is to be jumped in the alley, smacked around a bit, pushed behind the dumpster, and taught what life on the streets is really like. Bring your friends and pass me around like a cell-block sissy—I don't mind.

A SECRET MOST OTHERS DON'T KNOW ABOUT ME: I was married to a queen for three days in my youth. (I ran off during the honeymoon.)

MY MOTTO: I need a tom who can make every day Christmas.

SEX KITTENS 154

THE ORIGINAL MAGGIE THE CAT

WHAT I'M LOOKING FOR: PWT in prime of his life wants strapping young PAT to rescue me from the tedium of day-to-day life. I need to get out and take a good drink from life's water dish. Be my hero and get me off of this hot tin roof!

WHY YOU WANT TO GET TO KNOW ME: I have a lot of experience and I'm eager to impart it on the willing ears and heart of a bright, attentive tom. I've got more money than Peggy Guggenheim and more free time than Joan Crawford's kids had bruises. I'm on the board of the local museum.

MY IDEAL DATE INCLUDES: Anything you want, honey, so long as it means spending some nice quality time together, preferably in private. You could spend the entire evening cleaning yourself and I wouldn't mind, so long as you look good doing it and let me watch!

A SECRET MOST OTHERS DON'T KNOW ABOUT ME: Sometimes, when I feel like my life's gone to the litterbox, I crank call local support group hotlines and see how long I can keep them on the phone.

MY MOTTO: It's so very, very hot in here!

Meow!

SEX KITTENS 155

Doll Collector Seeks Fellow Afficionados!

WHAT I'M LOOKING FOR: Mature PWT iso CA/WT with similar interests (collectibles, dolls, antiquing) to share activities with. Must enjoy long weekends spent searching for rare, overlooked pieces at estate sales.

WHY YOU WANT TO GET TO KNOW ME: I'm a financially secure, down-to-earth tom with a good home. I think that, like all fine antiques, my patina only makes me more valuable. Maybe I'm no longer mint, but I've been well-preserved and it shows.

WHAT I'M READING/WATCHING: I watch *Antiques Road Show* and *Murder She Wrote*. I subscribe to *Antique Doll Collector* and *Country Collectibles*.

I'M MOST NEUROTIC ABOUT: I have a recurring nightmare where I wake up and find that all the furniture in the house has been scratched up beyond repair—and there's veneer under my claws.

MY MOTTO: I'm like an original '64 Miss Barbie: worth a fortune, fully poseable, and featuring fully functional "sleepy eyes."

Karaoke Champions Unite!

From: tom10001
Sent: Monday, July 18, 2005 @ 4:13 PM
To: CWT
Subject: RE: Karaoke Champions Unite!

WHAT I'M LOOKING FOR: CWT auditioning for gold-throated CW toms bitten by the showbiz bug, to provide harmony and backup. If you're good, I'll even let you sing lead every once in a while.

WHY YOU WANT TO GET TO KNOW ME: I'm a born performer who loves to be the center of attention! I'm confident and easy to please. I love toms who don't feel threatened and don't play mind games.

WHAT I'M READING/LISTENING TO/WATCHING: I can watch *Moulin Rouge* over and over again, especially the duets between Nicole Kidman (a goddess!) and Ewan MacGregor (my husband!). Other movies I love: *Cabaret, Mame,* the good parts of *Yentl.* Last book I read: the Paris Hilton's *Confessions of an Heiress.* Favorite music: the song stylings of Kiki & Herb.

I'M MOST NEUROTIC ABOUT: No more "Just Jack!" jokes, please.

MY MOTTO: Herrrrre's Romeow!!!

SEX
KITTENS
157

Let's Swap Spit

WHAT I'M LOOKING FOR: CAT looking for no-attitude CA/WT who wants to cut the small talk and get straight to the good stuff.

WHY YOU WANT TO GET TO KNOW ME: Under my tough exterior beats the heart of a field mouse—but only because I swallowed him whole. I have a quick temper, and when it flares up, I want to be left alone, no exceptions! But if you earn my respect, I will always treat you like an equal, or better.

BEST/WORST/BIGGEST LIE I EVER TOLD: My first boyfriend was insecure in bed, and rightly so, but I had him convinced he was the greatest lover on the block. (And then I broke up with him.)

A SECRET MOST OTHERS DON'T KNOW ABOUT ME: Sometimes I like to roll around in toilet paper and pretend I'm a Persian.

MY MOTTO:
"Here kitty kitty"
my ass.

SEXY FELINE
MACHINE!

SEX
KITTENS
158

I'm Fierce and You're Flirtatious

What I'm Looking For:
CWT iso CAT who'll make good prey.
I love to hunt and chase; you love
to be stalked by a strong, crazy tom
who won't rest until he gets what
he came for.

**Why You Want To Get To
Know Me:** I like to think of
myself as a domesticated wildcat.
I can take or leave the lush life—
indoor beds, plenty of cat food,
fresh water—and I actually enjoy
spending long weekends roaming
free from my captors, only to
return when I'm good and ready.

My Ideal Date Includes:
We meet. Sniff each other out.
With a sudden growl and a hiss, you take off running. I pursue, chasing you
over dressers and under beds, until I tackle you with a jump and bite you into
submission.

My Favorite Physical Activities: Scaring the children. Making
the toddler cry, then leaving the room before I can be blamed for it.

My Motto: Don't get a ticket if you're afraid of the ride.

Hunky Stud!

SEX
KITTENS
159

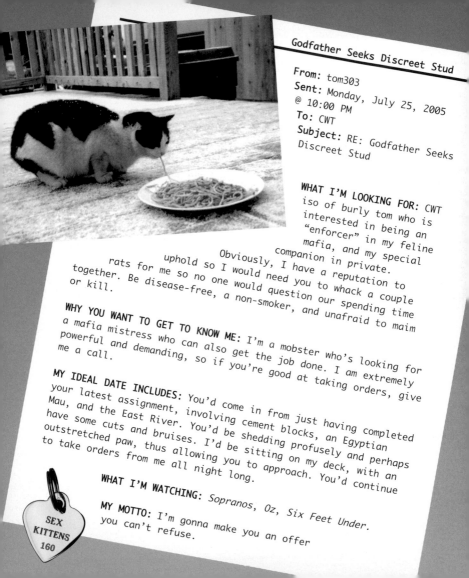

Godfather Seeks Discreet Stud

From: tom303
Sent: Monday, July 25, 2005 @ 10:00 PM
To: CWT
Subject: RE: Godfather Seeks Discreet Stud

WHAT I'M LOOKING FOR: CWT iso of burly tom who is interested in being an "enforcer" in my feline mafia, and my special companion in private. Obviously, I have a reputation to uphold so I would need you to whack a couple rats for me so no one would question our spending time together. Be disease-free, a non-smoker, and unafraid to maim or kill.

WHY YOU WANT TO GET TO KNOW ME: I'm a mobster who's looking for a mafia mistress who can also get the job done. I am extremely powerful and demanding, so if you're good at taking orders, give me a call.

MY IDEAL DATE INCLUDES: You'd come in from just having completed your latest assignment, involving cement blocks, an Egyptian Mau, and the East River. You'd be shedding profusely and perhaps have some cuts and bruises. I'd be sitting on my deck, with an outstretched paw, thus allowing you to approach. You'd continue to take orders from me all night long.

WHAT I'M WATCHING: Sopranos, Oz, Six Feet Under.

MY MOTTO: I'm gonna make you an offer you can't refuse.

SEX
KITTENS
160

NIGHTSHIFT PROGRAMMER NEEDS DEBUGGING

WHAT I'M LOOKING FOR: CWT geek iso same, for friendship, activities, maybe more. We both know first-hand what it's like to spend long hours in front of a monitor. I want someone who's interested in going offline and roughing it every once in a while—you know, spending the night outdoors, digging in the trash for food, chasing neighborhood dogs, and tormenting the birds.

WHY YOU WANT TO GET TO KNOW ME: I'm smart, funny, and a little silly when I get tired. I can recite every line of the *Star Wars* trilogy.

MY IDEAL DATE INCLUDES: Back-to-back viewings of *Akira* and *Ghost in the Shell*, followed by long, excited conversations over Red Bull or coffee (your choice).

WHAT I'M READING/LISTENING TO/WATCHING: Currently devouring Volume 3 of Neal Stephenson's *Baroque Cycle*, *The System of the World*. Listening to Gorillaz, Chemlab, old NIN when it's really late and I'm getting sleepy.

MY MOTTO: Always take the red pill.

SEX KITTENS 161

Museum-Quality Piece
Seeks Ear Nibbler

WHAT I'M LOOKING FOR: PWT needs devoted, educated, sophisticated PA/WT to provide sexual satisfaction. Must love biting and nibbling and must be willing to hold me post-coitus. As a hairless cat, I get cold easily, and I'd like to avoid having to put on my sweater, lovely as it is.

WHY YOU WANT TO GET TO KNOW ME: I'm a rare specimen of feline perfection. I may look fragile, but I can get pretty wild. My ears have so many nerve endings, just the thought of a strapping young tom coming near them makes my pads sweat.

WHAT'S IN MY BEDROOM: An afghan, a small electric blanket, pillows, booties for my paws when there's a draft, and lots more sweaters (hand-picked for me by my color-blind, fashion-challenged, high-functioning dimwit of a human). And let's not forget earmuffs, which are invaluable in the winter.

I'M MOST NEUROTIC ABOUT: There's a rumor going around that my mother was actually a bat and I am the result of an experiment in cross-species breeding.

MY MOTTO: A little ear nibble goes a long way.

Purr-fect!

SEX
KITTENS
162

Songwriter Seeks Muse

What I'm Looking For: I'm a CAT in the big city trying to make ends meet while working on my sure-to-be-a-hit show, *Pads, Paws, and Whiskers.*

Why You Want To Get To Know Me: I'm usually a lot of fun to be around, but constant work has made my social life about as fun as John Cage's *4' 33"* played in an empty concert hall. All this solo time has given me writer's block and I need to get out and have a little fun to get back my ear for melody.

What I'm Reading/Watching: Favorite movies include *M. Butterfly* and *The Crying Game.* Currently reading *Everything Was Possible: The Birth of the Musical "Follies,"* by Ted Chapin.

I'm Most Neurotic About: The maddeningly repetitive tune of the ice cream truck, which comes around here three times a day in the summer.

My Motto: Play your sorrows in a major chord and nobody will know they're sorrows.

From: tom5
Sent: Tuesday, July 5, 2005 @ 10:45 PM
To: CAT
Subject: RE: Amatuer Marine Biologist Seeks Same for Undersea Adventures

WHAT I'M LOOKING FOR: I'm a shy, well-educated CWT who is fascinated by fish of all kinds—for study, not for eating. I'm looking for an intimate friend and lab partner for fun times and specimen gathering trips. Absolutely no fish-eaters! (Yes, you heard correctly.) Must not get seasick.

WHY YOU WANT TO GET TO KNOW ME: After spending years being embarrassed about my passion for ichthyology, I've finally accepted that this is my true calling. If you are my kindred spirit, you don't have to hide your love for these amazing creatures any longer.

WHAT I'M READING: The Secret Life of Lobsters, The Voyage of the Beagle, Eco's The Island of the Day Before.

MY MOTTO: Go fish!

SEX KITTENS 164

SEXY FELINE MACHINE!

PERSONALS

TRUST FUND TOM SEEKS PARAMOUR FOR STYLISH MISBEHAVIN'

WHAT I'M LOOKING FOR: CWT iso handsome and sensual PWT able to keep up with my extravagant spending habits. Should know the basics of finer living: which small animals are in season, how to drink water without dipping your paw in, etc. Not interested in cats with champagne tastes but beer-bottle pockets.

WHY YOU WANT TO GET TO KNOW ME: I'm a wealthy, healthy tom with a lot of stamina and energy. I have extensive experience in living the good life. I spend most of my days lounging around by the pool and making "friends" with new toms in the neighborhood.

A SECRET MOST OTHERS DON'T KNOW ABOUT ME: I once posed for *Tomcat* magazine just for the hell of it, but I wore a mask to protect my family's name and my reputation.

I'M MOST NEUROTIC ABOUT: I don't like it when strays wander onto the property and start poaching my voles.

MY MOTTO: I made money the old-old-fashioned way: I inherited it.

SEX KITTENS 165

QUEENS
SEEKING
QUEENS

(Bi-)Curious? Let Me Out of the Bag

WHAT I'M LOOKING FOR: CWQ searching for a curious CAQ who's into all cats, regardless of plumbing. Must be open-minded, loving, and trusting. Looking for friendship or relationship. Please be unattached if considering anything romantic—I don't want to be the "other queen" in your life.

WHY YOU WANT TO GET TO KNOW ME: You can confide in me. I'll keep your darkest secrets under wraps. Wanna know more? You'll have to contact me personally for details, but I promise you won't be disappointed.

MY IDEAL DATE INCLUDES: Too many cats rush into things these days. I'd like to get to know you first, and if we turn out to be better as friends, that's great, no hard feelings. So, for an ideal first date I'd want to just hang out and get to know each other as we play around a little.

**WHAT I'M LISTEN-
ING TO/WATCHING:**
The L Word is the
best! I listen to Fiona
Apple, Alicia Keys,
anything and every-
thing by Stevie Nicks.

MY MOTTO: "Give to
me your leather, take
from me
my lace."

SEX
KITTENS
168

The Heart Is a Lonely Hunter

What I'm Looking For: CWQ iso P/CA/WQ. You be a literary adventurer who's as at home hunting grasshoppers as you are curling up on a good book.

Why You Want To Get To Know Me: I'm the strong, silent type. I love a good conversation so long as I'm the one doing most of the listening. I'm very independent, but I appreciate the company of a fine queen by my side.

What I'm Reading/Listening To: My favorite bands are Sleater-Kinney, The Butchies, Le Tigre—and I'll always have a soft spot in my heart for the Indigo Girls. Currently re-reading Willa Cather's novels (*My Antonia* is my all-time favorite). Can't get through any Gertrude Stein, but my water dish is a coffee mug with her face on it.

A Secret Most Others Don't Know About Me: I was voted "Most likely to be entered into shows" in my litter.

My Motto: Still waters run deep.

Call Tonight!

SEX KITTENS 169

Tears of a Clown

From: queen939
Sent: Friday, April 29, 2005 @ 1:25 AM
To: PWQ
Subject: RE: Tears of a Clown

WHAT I'M LOOKING FOR: CWQ iso PWQ. I need a level-headed soul mate to calm my party-going ways and ground me in a harmonious relationship of love and tenderness: no drama, no games, no manipulation. Want to build a lasting bond based on 80% trust and 20% lust.

WHY YOU WANT TO GET TO KNOW ME: I'm tired of being the happy-go-lucky gal who never acts like she has a bad day. You must be willing to take the grr with the purr and still love me in the morning. I can definitely be moody, but I can also be under-standing and caring when you get down in the dumps, and I'll do whatever it takes to improve your mood.

I'M MOST NEUROTIC ABOUT: My mascara running.

A SECRET MOST OTHERS DON'T KNOW ABOUT ME: Clowns terrify me.

MY MOTTO: "Isn't it rich, aren't we a pair?"

PERSONALS

I KNOW HOW THE CAGED BIRD TASTES

WHAT I'M LOOKING FOR: CWQ needs a life partner ready to spend the golden years with a sensible, giant-hearted queen who's tired of being a wife and mother. Prefer P/CWQ at least ten years or older, down to earth, not too pampered, who enjoys breaking the rules every now and then. Similar experience with raising families a bit of a plus.

WHY YOU WANT TO GET TO KNOW ME: I'm a momma queen who realized late in life that she wanted a lot more than any tom could provide. Now that I've "come out of the cage," I feel like a ten-month-old kit as I start over in my new role as single feline first, mother second, and victim last. I'm warm, incredibly patient, thick-skinned, and I know what I want. (At last!)

WHAT'S IN MY BEDROOM: Photos of my seven litters—that's 44 children in all, and more than 1,200 grandchildren by my last estimate!

WHAT I'M WATCHING: I love game shows. I usually start with *Wheel of Fortune*, to warm up, then move on to *Jeopardy!*, where the real fun begins—I use a pen and paper and track my score along with the TV. I also enjoy watching Paula Poundstone, and I have all of her specials on tape.

MY MOTTO: It's never too late to start over!

SEX KITTENS
171

Single City Cat Wants
Sexy Downstairs Neighbor

WHAT I'M LOOKING FOR: CAQ iso an urban sophisticate CAQ
who loves life in the city and wants a partner for fun, clubbing,
and maybe (almost definitely) more. You: be confident, well-
educated, and eager to explore the city with a sister-in-crime.

WHY YOU WANT TO GET TO KNOW ME: I'm an energetic little
she-tiger who really knows how to paint the town in tiger stripes.
Let me play Rhoda to your Mary Tyler Moore, Kate to your Allie,
and I'll prove it.

WHAT'S IN MY BEDROOM: I've got the typical tiny city apartment,
which half the time is in use by humans so I can't get in.
(Although sometimes they leave me a sock or two.)
Other than sleeping there I hardly
ever use it, so I like to think of the
rest of the city as my extended
bedroom.

**WHAT I'M READING/LISTENING
TO/WATCHING:** On TV: *The Daily
Show*, when my Tivo thinks to
record it. Reading: whatever Candace
Bushnell has put out most recently.
Guilty pleasure: The Dixie Chicks.

MY MOTTO: A good pedicure can
fix anything.

SEX
KITTENS
172

Meow!

East Meets West

What I'm Looking For: PAQ wants to find sincere, elegant PAQ to bridge the cultural divide. I'm a Bombay, you be a Maine Coon or American Wirehair, with papers, natch. Sorry, no mixes or crossbreeds.

Why You Want To Get To Know Me: I have a sleek, silky coat and I love to have it cleaned, sometimes for hours. I have very refined tastes and will accept nothing but the best, whether it's food, bedding, or romance.

What I'm Reading/ Watching: Reruns of *I Dream of Jeannie*. The last movie I saw was *Monsoon Wedding*. I'm currently re-reading the *Bhagavad Gita*.

A Secret Most Others Don't Know About Me: I'm an accomplished sitar player.

My Motto: I'll be the flower, you be the willow.

Domestic and Desperate

From: queen69
Sent: Sunday, July 31, 2005 @ 7:56 PM
To: PA/WQ
Subject: RE: Domestic and Desperate

WHAT I'M LOOKING FOR: PA/W queen who can break this CWQ out of her consumerist prison. I want to get away from all of this, grab life by the throat and shake it till it stops squeaking. If that appeals to you, contact me—you can be the Thelma to my Louise!

WHY YOU WANT TO GET TO KNOW ME: I'm a warrior spirit trapped in a world that places a premium on cute. I have everything I thought I could ever want—and I've never been more bored. Looking for a queen who's not materialistic, who's generous with her time, maybe even a bit sassy.

WHAT I'M WATCHING: I watch *Another World* and *Days of Our Lives* religiously. I still can't believe they tried to convince us that Marlena was a serial killer.

BEST/WORST/BIGGEST LIE I EVER TOLD: I got married and had a litter of kittens because I thought the tom lived in a nice house and I wanted to live there.

MY MOTTO: Good sex is better than any shopping spree, and cheaper, too.

SEX KITTENS 174

PERSONALS

DESPERATE HOUSEPETS DATING SERVICE

SPORTS LOVER WANTS CHEERLEADER

WHAT I'M LOOKING FOR: CWQ wants a peppy PAQ between two and four years old to keep me entertained during halftime, and to help me relax after the game.

WHY YOU WANT TO GET TO KNOW ME: I'm a husky beauty, gruff but sensuous. Think of me as the feline Kathleen Turner. I'm very physically active, and I want a special friend who can keep up with me, or at least urge me to do my best both on the field and off.

MY IDEAL DATE INCLUDES: You'd come watch me play rugby, then hang out and meet my girlfriends (all of whom have to approve of you, of course).

WHAT I'M READING/WATCHING: I watch every WNBA game they televise. Currently reading *Tall Enough to Coach*, by Marsha Sharp.

MY MOTTO: Let's play ball!

SEX KITTENS 175

Vocalist Needs Accompanist

WHAT I'M LOOKING FOR: I'm a romantic, music-loving PAQ looking for a P/CAQ with talented paws to provide a melodic counterpoint to my high-strung personality. I'm a hothouse flower who needs careful attention—and lots of it—to flourish, so you'd better love to pamper high-maintenance queens. You should

know that tuna makes me barf. Come to think of it, just about everything makes me barf.

WHY YOU WANT TO GET TO KNOW ME: I can be haughty and hard to please, but if you're the right queen you will appreciate my every precious mood. I have a piercingly beautiful singing voice that never fails to get a reaction from humans.

WHAT I'M READING/LISTENING TO/WATCHING: I just read *The Da Vinci Code* (hasn't everyone?) and am digging into the new *Harry Potter* book. I like all different kinds of music, but I'm particularly fond of Chinese Opera. I like to sing along.

A SECRET MOST OTHERS DON'T KNOW ABOUT ME: My owners give me half a Paxil tablet every morning.

MY MOTTO: But I already *took* a chill pill!

A Surprise in Every Box!

From: queen5091
Sent: Friday, July 1, 2005 @ 10:14 AM
To: CAQ
Subject: RE: A Surprise in Every Box!

WHAT I'M LOOKING FOR: CAQ seeks same for amorous adventures. You must like surprises and be able to help me get out of tight situations. I want a friend first, a lover second, and someone who can bail me out third. Must enjoy late-night excursions into forbidden nooks and crannies. Please be good with your paws and be declawed or recently trimmed.

WHY YOU ~~WANT TO GET TO KNOW~~ ME: I'm an energetic risk-taker who's not afraid to jump in headfirst, even if I'm not sure there's water in the pool. My curiosity knows no bounds: if you've ever wondered what's at the bottom of that box or under all that dirt in the planter, we just might be soul mates.

WHAT'S IN MY BEDROOM: A cache of toys stolen from the kids' bedrooms, several piles of insect carapaces, and a jack-in-the-box (I know what's in there but I just can't resist!).

MY MOTTO: Seize the day!

SEX
KITTENS
177

Female Gamer in Search of Real-World Contact

WHAT I'M LOOKING FOR: CAQ needs to establish contact with a PA/WQ in the meatspace for companionship and tutoring. I need someone who can introduce me to the ways of feline love. You be young and tech-savvy. You must enjoy gaming (or, frankly, we'll have nothing to talk about). Bonus points for queens with their own WOW accounts.

WHY YOU WANT TO GET TO KNOW ME: I'm a hardcore gamer who's a newbie to romance. I have quick reflexes and I love puzzles—complicated situations excite me. I would love to try to pry out your secrets as we cuddle together on top of my GenCon T-shirt.

WHAT'S IN MY BEDROOM: *Lord of the Rings* box set, PS2, a picture of Angelina Jolie as Lara Croft that I chewed out of a magazine.

A SECRET MOST OTHERS DON'T KNOW ABOUT ME: I'm three years old and still a virgin.

MY MOTTO:
Fraggers
make
twitchy
lovers.

SEX
KITTENS
178

Lipstick Pussycat Shopping for the Perfect Accessory

What I'm Looking For: CAQ wants to meet CA/WQ for shopping, eating, and unmentionable after-hours fun. You be stylish, flashy, proud of your appearance but not too vain.

Why You Want To Get To Know Me: I'm a sweet queen with a killer smile and beautiful orange eyes that have been known to drive both toms and queens wild. I love to hunt—for the perfect purchase, that is. Happiness to me is discovering an unadvertised sale at that perfect boutique.

My Ideal Date Includes: You'd come over as soon as my doors open and take advantage of my "half-off" sale. Just remember: if you break it, you buy it.

A Secret Most Others Don't Know About Me: Once, on a dare, I made out with a ferret.

My Motto: Only amateurs buy things at full price.

SEXY FELINE MACHINE!

From: queen9945
Sent: Sunday, August 7, 2005 @ 9:36 PM
To: PA/WQ
Subject: RE: Tennis Pro Recruiting Ball Girl

WHAT I'M LOOKING FOR: Old PAQ iso young PA/WQ—a kit who's a tennis enthusiast, to learn at the feet of a self-taught master of the clay court. Be nimble, lithe, look good both in a tennis skirt and out of one.

WHY YOU WANT TO GET TO KNOW ME: I'm hard but fair. I like to teach, and I'll give you an education money can't buy (it's not even legal to pay for the kind of education I'm going to give you). Be prepared for a long, hard workout with me—you'll probably end up going home a little sore.

MY DREAM VACATION: I would kill to spend a week at Wimbledon, especially if I could see Svetlana Kuznetsova in action.

I'M MOST NEUROTIC ABOUT: Losing my reflexes; getting tennis elbow.

MY MOTTO: Tennis anyone?

SEX KITTENS 180

P E R S O N A L S

LET ME HAVE SOME OF YOUR GOOD LUCK

WHAT I'M LOOKING FOR: CAQ iso an all natural, all white queen (no bleach-jobs) who can help rid me of the curse of bad luck. Please be patient and pure of heart.

WHY YOU WANT TO GET TO KNOW ME: As a black cat I have been cursed all my life. My owner looks like a witch and all other humans run away from me. I can't have litters (I tried multiple times with the tom next door—just for the sake of having kittens, not because I liked him—and I never got pregnant), my fur is always matted, and I hardly ever land on my feet. Is there a queen out there who can help reverse my unfortunate fortune?

WHAT I'M READING: *Create Your Own Luck: 8 Principles of Attracting Good Fortune in Life, Love, and Work* and *Morality, Moral Luck and Responsibility: Fortune's Web.* Neither seems to be helping much.

I'M MOST NEUROTIC ABOUT: Standing under ladders, breaking a mirror, and stepping on cracks in the sidewalk—I don't need to compound my bad luck. Also, I get very nervous on Friday the 13th.

MY MOTTO: I'm really not a demon in disguise.

SEX KITTENS 181

Butch Babe Needs Lovely Lady

WHAT I'M LOOKING FOR: PWQ iso lipstick C/PA/WQ who wants to be treated like a lady. I know toms don't treat you right, but I will. I'm a queen too; I know what we want.

WHY YOU WANT TO GET TO KNOW ME: I've been taking testosterone hormones for over a year now so I am pretty manly. But not too manly to be sensitive and caring. I recently started growing enough hair to have a whisker mustache, do you like it?

MY FAVORITE PHYSICAL ACTIVITIES: I love to pump iron, play football, wrestle, and pleasure you all night long.

WHAT'S IN MY BEDROOM: My leather jacket, a bandana, and a top-notch collection of cat-sized chaps.

MY MOTTO: Who said toms had more fun?

SEX KITTENS 182

I'll Be Your Secret Lover

From: queen6379
Sent: Friday, April 29, 2005 @ 1:25 AM
To: P/CWQ
Subject: RE: I'll Be Your Secret Lover

WHAT I'M LOOKING FOR:
CWQ iso married but curious CWQ who wants to dip her paw into the world of queen-on-queen erotic play. I prefer large, young queens, who are inquisitive, very clean, and ready to try new things.

WHY YOU WANT TO GET TO KNOW ME: I'm discreet—nobody will ever find out your secret with me—and a lot of fun. I'll help you discover feelings you didn't know you had, and reach places your tom doesn't know how to reach. I'm very safe and will never try anything that makes either one of us feel uncomfortable.

MY IDEAL DATE INCLUDES: I'm easy. Just keep me nearby—in a cabinet, a suitcase, on the roof, in a hole, whatever—and then drop by whenever you feel like it for some one-on-one all-lady tongue fighting.

A SECRET MOST OTHERS DON'T KNOW ABOUT ME: I'm not really black all over, but I'll leave that for to you to discover....

MY MOTTO: Nobody needs to know.

SEX
KITTENS
183

You Are Getting Very Sleepy

WHAT I'M LOOKING FOR: A C/PAQ who will allow me to practice my hypnosis skills on her. If you will just relax, I'll take you on a magical journey to your past lives and lead you to a greater understanding of yourself and the world.

WHY YOU WANT TO GET TO KNOW ME: I was trained in the art of hypnotism by the famous mesmerist Dr. Felis Catus. I used to be skeptical, until I finally gave in and let her take me back to my third life as a liger. She had me roaring so loudly the cat next door came to see what was going on.

IN MY BEDRROM: A gold pocket watch, a wooden disc with a spiral on it, candles, and a cage (in case my patients get nasty).

I'M MOST NEUROTIC ABOUT: Someone inspecting my certificate from Dr. Felis Catus too closely.

MY MOTTO: Look into my eyes...

Call Tonight!

SEX KITTENS 184

My Rhythm Is Gonna Get You

What I'm looking for:
Athletic CAQ iso leggy bombshell CAQ to be dancing partner and more. You be limber, well-toned, perfectly proportioned, short-haired. Music affects you on an unconscious level—you can't help but move to it. Let's choreograph a hot number that leaves us both spent and exhausted!

Why You Want To Get To Know Me: I'm a malure (10 year-old) queen who's been active my whole life. In great shape.

What I'm Reading/Listening To/Watching: I love old musicals, especially *West Side Story*, *Singin' in the Rain*, *Top Hat* and *Swing Time*. Favorite musical style: big band, especially Glen Miller. Enjoy watching Lawrence Welk reruns on PBS and any televised ballroom dancing competitions.

A Secret Most Others Don't Know About Me: I secretly also like hip-hop. I'd die for Mos Def.

My Motto: "You make me feel like dancin'."

Photographer Wants to Develop a Relationship

WHAT I'M LOOKING FOR: Do you wanna be in pictures? CAQ searching for PA/WQ for personal project. Must be more than beautiful; my jaded eye can see past the surface and needs something deeper. Should be between 2 and 4 years old, petite, shorthair. No orange cats, sorry.

WHY YOU WANT TO GET TO KNOW ME: I have a good eye, and I can make anyone look beautiful in front of the camera. But what I really want is someone who's beautiful in real life.

MY IDEAL DATE INCLUDES: You'd show up at my studio after hours for a private photo shoot. No props, no costumes, just you and me and my camera in an intimate, private setting where all our inhibitions disappear. If things go well, I'd take you to the darkroom for some extra special one-on-one time.

A SECRET MOST OTHERS DON'T KNOW ABOUT ME: I never destroy the negatives...

MY MOTTO: The camera always lies.

SEX KITTENS 186

PERSONALS
DESPERATE HOUSEPETS DATING SERVICE

TWO MOMS CAN MAKE A RIGHT

WHAT I'M LOOKING FOR: Recently divorced CWQ iso CA/WQ who knows what it feels like to come from a large family and wants to start one of her own with a warm, level-headed queen. Any breed is fine, but please be between 2 and 6 years old. Lutheran background a plus.

WHY YOU WANT TO GET TO KNOW ME: I'm the middle kit of a litter of nine, and we all grew up together on a farm in the Midwest. I love the company of other cats—the more the merrier, as far as I'm concerned. Love to share. No kittens from previous marriage, so I'd love to get started on our own brood soon.

WHAT'S IN MY BEDROOM: Very little these days—he took it all in the divorce. But that's okay because I want to make a clean start with a queen who will help me build a family of my own.

MY FAVORITE PHYSICAL ACTIVITIES: I love cookouts—the smell of the grill, the food that inevitably hits the ground. Also love to go running, not only over furniture but, through the urban wilderness.

MY MOTTO: The most beautiful sound in the world is a kitten's first mew.

SEX KITTENS 187

No Attachments, Just Fun

WHAT I'M LOOKING FOR: High-spirited CAQ iso same for fun and games. Not looking for anything long-term or too serious. I'm young and just want to have a little fun with a queen with similar interests. You be athletic, self-confident, competitive, good-

hearted, have a great smile. Be able to tell a good joke and hold your own in conversation—a meower, not a yawner. No prudes.

WHY YOU WANT TO GET TO KNOW ME: I'll try anything if you dare me. I have a very long, very muscular tongue, and I love to share it with friends.

MY FAVORITE PHYSICAL ACTIVITIES: Running, jumping, chasing—pretty much any physical activity. Love to go to the park and pick fights with dogs on leashes, or walk past backyards and rub my scent against the fences to drive the dogs on the other side crazy.

BEST/WORST/BIGGEST LIE I EVER TOLD: I once pretended to be pregnant to scare off this tom who had an obsessive crush on me. Unfortunately it didn't work, and I had to beat him up pretty badly to get him to leave me alone, but that was still the biggest lie I ever told.

MY MOTTO: You won't know if you like something until you give it at least one lick.

SEX KITTENS 188

Hottie!

Need a Teddy Cat

From: queen1031
Sent: Friday, August 2, 2005 @ 11:49 AM
To: P/CWQ
Subject: RE: Need a Teddy Cat

WHAT I'M LOOKING FOR: Dainty CWQ iso a P/CWQ who can be my friend and playmate. Not interested in anything else right now—if we like hanging out, let's give it awhile and see if it grows into something more.

WHY YOU WANT TO GET TO KNOW ME: I'm in an awkward phase right now due to another growth spurt—big feet and tiny head. But I'm sure that will change soon. Can be very catty, but if I'm grumpy, just wait five minutes and I'll be back to normal again.

WHAT I'M READING/WATCHING: I watch *Ellen* every day, and also *Fear Factor!* Love to read both *Kitten Fancy* and *Cat Fancy* magazines.

MY IDEAL DATE INCLUDES: A lot of stuff. You'd help me scratch up the human legs that are all around us. We'd play "kill the ribbon," then swat at our reflections in the bathroom mirror. I also enjoy climbing inside of pillowcases and then trying to claw my way out the other end.

MY MOTTO: Yippee!

SEX KITTENS 189

Free Radical Seeks Others to Help Buck the System

What I'm Looking For: CAQ iso fellow warrior queens, any breed or mix fine, A/W not an issue, to join me in the great cause against tomcat oppression. You be strong, dedicated, focused not flighty, not interested in starting a family. Debutantes not needed or welcome.

Why You Want To Get To Know Me: I'm a fiery former street cat who's life is never boring. I love to shake things up, get in toms' faces and let them know a penis doesn't make you all-powerful. I enjoy ransacking the yards of uptight neighbors and getting into "inappropriate" situations that horrify the status quo cats.

What's In My Bedroom: Signed, framed photograph of Jean O'Leary, my shelf of Marlene Dietrich biographies, an extensive collection of vibrators, posters of Two Nice Girls and Janis Joplin.

I'm Most Neurotic About: I know it's unlikely, but I still have panic attacks about finding myself suddenly pregnant.

My Motto: Pussy power now!

Looking for Ms. Right Meow

WHAT I'M LOOKING FOR: PAQ iso of P/CA/WQ immediately for good times. I only have two criteria: you're not picky and you've got the right parts. Other, less important qualities: be docile and willing, not a tease, and no fatties. Oh, also be disease free.

WHY YOU WANT TO GET TO KNOW ME: I'm a busy cat with lots of fur to clean and lots of attention to receive. I don't have a lot of time for "romance." I want sex, and I want it when I say I want it, not after I take you to dinner or pretend to care about what you did earlier today. That's not rude, it's refreshingly honest—admit it.

MY IDEAL DATE INCLUDES: What do you think?

WHAT I'M LISTENING TO/WATCHING: Listening to the Yeah Yeah Yeahs, Patty Smythe, Sahara Hotnights, the Arcade Fire. Watching *The Wire* and *Deadwood.*

MY MOTTO: Start licking, I haven't got all day.

Meow!

SEX
KITTENS
191

From: tom2357
Sent: Friday, April 29, 2005 @ 1:25 AM
To: CA/WTQ
Subject: RE: Tough Cookie Needs Makeover, Possibly Rehab

WHAT I'M LOOKING FOR: Young CWT wants a momma cat (CA/WTQ) who's not easily threatened by anything, not surprised by anything, and used to dealing with problem cats, to provide care and guidance to a kitten who's had a rough start in life. No kittiphiles, please.

WHY YOU WANT TO GET TO KNOW ME: Though I'm now in a foster home, I'm still an alley cat at heart. Want to make a good impression on the folks and figured having a life coach like you couldn't hurt. I'm a diamond in the rough!

MY IDEAL DATE INCLUDES: I would love a play date that featured a good long bath, especially behind the ears. Also, I need to learn how to use that litter box thingie (why can't I just use the houseplants?) and what not to destroy when I'm practicing my fighting skills.

I'M MOST NEUROTIC ABOUT: Kicking the H was hard enough, but I'm afraid I'm never going to be able to give up the smokes!

MY MOTTO: "Tell St. Peter at the gate/That he'll just have to wait/While you smoke, smoke, smoke that cigarette!"

SEX KITTENS 194

HARD-LUCK KITTEN

WHAT I'M LOOKING FOR:
CWT wants big brother
or sister, CW/A, with a
good home and plenty
of room to share. Prefer
large farm or house
with lots of hiding
places.

**WHY YOU WANT TO GET
TO KNOW ME:** I don't
take up much space—
I'm small and quiet and
really nice. I'm pretty
self-sufficient, too,
though I sometimes
need help grooming
those hard-to-lick
places (due to my
abnormally small tongue).

WHAT'S IN MY BEDROOM: An occasional pebble, some sock lint, and
a pretty constant stink.

MY FAVORITE PHYSICAL ACTIVITIES: Sleeping on a real pillow. Also, eating
till my belly is bloated up like a swollen tick, then sleeping it off.

MY MOTTO: You don't know a person till you've lived in his shoe,
and then you probably know him a little too well.

SEX
KITTENS
195

Wanted: Big Beauty for Pressing Business

WHAT I'M LOOKING FOR: Horn-dog CAT wants plus-size P/CA/WQ for sensual play involving your beautiful big body and gravity. Seriously, I want to have to struggle to take a breath. You: BIG.

WHY YOU WANT TO GET TO KNOW ME: I'm a healthy, normal tom, disease-free, physically fit, who happens to have a yen for being sat on by fat queens. Does that make me a bad tom? I'm very loyal and faithful, and will get behind—or rather, beneath—my special queen no matter what she chooses to do in life.

MY IDEAL DATE INCLUDES: I'd love to take you to dinner and feed you a huge meal—filet mignon, poached salmon, foie gras, fettuccini alfredo, hamster, you name it. I'd eat a light salad or a bit of dried cat food, to avoid unpleasant vomiting later on in the evening. Then we'd retire to my room where I'd lie down on my side and you'd pass out on top of me, trapping me in exquisite agony for hours.

BEST/WORST/BIGGEST LIE I EVER TOLD: My ex-girlfriend was trying to lose weight, and I replaced all her "less active" dry food with high-calorie chow so she'd get even bigger.

MY MOTTO: Put that junk in the trunk and smother me with your love!

Call Tonight!

SEX KITTENS 196

Daisy Chain Needs Links

From: tom62357
Sent: Friday, August 19, 2005 @ 1:26 PM
To: Interested couple
Subject: RE: Daisy Chain Needs Links

WHAT WE'RE LOOKING FOR: Happily married CA tom and queen, looking for open-minded, healthy and happy similar CA couple eager to explore new sexual experiences with us. No unattached toms or queens, please. Must be mixed-gender couple. If either partner has any lines they won't cross, please detail in your letter. Photos a must.

WHY YOU WANT TO GET TO KNOW US: We're creative in the bedroom and love to explore new ideas. He: aggressive and dominant; sometimes bats around with the other team, but usually prefers queens. She: bohemian and playful, into role-playing, experienced in pleasing all cats regardless of gender.

WHAT'S IN OUR BEDROOM: Bed large enough for four, a little cat-nip (we're not nip-heads, but we like it every once in a while), smoked mirrors on one wall, a gold metallic orb floor lamp, plush brown carpet.

OUR IDEAL DATE INCLUDES: Come early, pick an identity for the evening from the costume closet, and leave your inhibitions behind for the next several hours.

OUR MOTTO: It's not cheating if your partner is in the bed, too.

SEX KITTENS 197

Lion Seeks Plushophile

From: roar21
Sent: Tuesday,
August 9, 2005 @ 6:14 PM
To: Plush-lover
Subject: RE: Lion Seeks Plushophile

WHAT I'M LOOKING FOR: Genderless stuffed lion seeks C/PA/WT/Q for constant companionship and gentle grooming. You: into the plushie/furry scene, loyal and kind. No freaks, please.

WHY YOU WANT TO GET TO KNOW ME: If you've ever looked in the mirror and thought, "Who's the king of the jungle? Me, that's who!" then you and I should talk. You'll think that every time you look into my beautiful brown glass eyes.

WHAT'S IN MY BEDROOM: I've been dumped by my former partner (into tigers now, apparently), so I am currently without a bedroom, which is definitely not how I like to live. You can come see me in the dumpster behind the Taco Bell on Main Street; please hurry, 'cause garbage day is Thursday.

I'M MOST NEUROTIC ABOUT: Being used as a scratching post. Affection is one thing, but I know some cats like to get a little rough with their dolls. Please treat me with care (dry-clean only!) and I'll reward you with a lifetime of love.

MY MOTTO: Can't get enough of that plushie stuff!

SEX
KITTENS
198

PERSONALS

BREATHLESS

WHAT I'M LOOKING FOR: PWQ into erotic suffocation seeks P/CA/WT for hot, consensual breath play. Must enjoy bags, heavy blankets, and creative prop use. Safe only!

WHY YOU WANT TO GET TO KNOW ME: I'm a sexy queen with long silky fur, which I keep immaculately groomed. Healthy and happy personality. Not seeking anything long-term or serious—just want sane, safe partners to play with.

WHAT'S IN MY BEDROOM: Scarves, belts, shoelaces, a jump rope, and several feet of yarn.

MY IDEAL DATE INCLUDES: Some cats think giving flowers, dead birds, or maybe half-chewed mouse parts make the best first impression. Not for me. I'd prefer you to show up with an empty fast food sack. I'll happily let you in, then stick my head inside the sack and huff until I'm dizzy.

MY MOTTO: I won't settle for a cat who doesn't take my breath away.

SEXY FELINE MACHINE !

SEX KITTENS 199

Look but Don't Touch

WHAT WE'RE LOOKING FOR: Two CA queens want to bring in another bi-curious CAQ as a voyeur only. You: be any breed or mix, between 4 and 12 years old, able to follow rules, and know how to be quiet and disappear when it's time to go.

WHY YOU WANT TO GET TO KNOW US: We're well-educated professionals, 7 and 9 years old, who can be very generous to the right queen. We don't want to date anyone, we just want to have a little fun with an appreciative audience.

OUR IDEAL DATE: We'd prefer to eschew the traditional romantic trappings, so any "date" would be no-frills only. Please eat beforehand. We'll say "hello," provide drinks, then leave while you get comfortable—there's a nice louvered closet in the bedroom, or you can climb into the hamper. We'll return, hot and filled with lust, and act like you aren't there.

A SECRET MOST OTHERS DON'T KNOW ABOUT US: We enjoy public coupling, and have been chased out of the prep kitchen at our local deli for our carnal exploits.

OUR MOTTO: Please turn off your cell phone. No smoking. And no meowing. Now, sit back and enjoy the show!

SEX KITTENS 200

Bathroom Buddies Itching for Attendant

From: TPtoms25
Sent: Friday, August 12, 2005 @ 7:12 PM
To: CAT
Subject: RE: Bathroom Buddies Itching for Attendant

WHAT WE'RE LOOKING FOR: Dirty T/T couple, both CA, want to be cleaned by a CA cross-dressing tom. You must be cute, and willing to lick us everywhere. Disease- and flea-free, please.

WHY YOU WANT TO GET TO KNOW US: We're both young, fit, attractive toms with strong personalities. We love to get good and dirty while playing, then spend the rest of the evening cleaning each other off—we thought it might be nice to add a tom with a slightly more feminine touch to the mix.

OUR FAVORITE PHYSICAL ACTIVITIES: When the lid's up: playing in the water. When it's down: shredding the paper.

WE'RE MOST NEUROTIC ABOUT: The bathtub. There's a difference between a turn-on (the sink) and a death trap (the tub). We never "do" the tub, so don't even ask.

OUR MOTTO: TP party tonight!

SEX KITTENS 201

Slave Badly Needs Training

WHAT I'M LOOKING FOR: CAT needs a master queen (P/C A/W, no preference) who will teach this disobedient slave who's the boss, even if that requires a well-positioned claw firmly pressed against the sensitive area where the family jewels used to be.

WHY YOU WANT TO GET TO KNOW ME: I'm ready and willing to obey the right queen, if she's ready to be my ultimate master. I'm a dirty boy who's slow to learn— I require LOTS of discipline.

WHAT'S IN MY BEDROOM: Harnesses, a small blindfold, a tail-cage, and my beloved home-made isolation box (see photo). But you're the boss, so if you'd prefer I live in a plastic lunch box, just tell me and I'll do it.

MY FAVORITE PHYSICAL ACTIVITIES: Catching your dinner for you. Covering the mess in your litter box until you're completely satisfied. Being sprayed with water. Accepting verbal abuse.

MY MOTTO: I am definitely NOT Spartacus.

SEX KITTENS 202

Wonder Twin Powers, Activate!

What We're Looking For: Twin PWTs iso limber and willing P/CAQ who's into being double-teamed by the two sexiest bachelors in town. You should be a perfectly proportioned young queen between 1 and 3 years old, with a long, narrow tail and long legs, eager to play.

Why You Want To Get To Know Us: We work out regularly, have totally awesome bodies, lots of stamina, and we work as a team. Our collaborative approach will leave you totally satisfied, that's our guarantee. We're 100% not gay.

Our Ideal Date Includes: We'd pick you up at 8 p.m., take you out to this great Italian place we know. Over dinner, we'd entertain you with stories of crazy adventures we've had. After a few drinks, we invite you back to our place. What happens next isn't something we can print in public, but let's just say you'd better do a lot of stretching and limbering up beforehand.

We're Most Neurotic About: Being mistaken for homosexuals— when was it ever a crime to look this good and be straight?

Our Motto: Double your pleasure!

SEX KITTENS 203

Traveling Trio Looking for Fourth

From: toms3
Sent: Monday, February 18, 2005 @ 6:11 AM
To: CA/WT
Subject: RE: Traveling Trio Looking for Fourth

WHAT WE'RE LOOKING FOR: We're three travelers, CWT/Q/Q, who plan on visiting every state in the union via UPS Ground. Looking for an adventure-hungry CA/WT to give us a fourth for the bridge table. No romantic payoff expected.

WHY YOU WANT TO GET TO KNOW US: We might be no-frills travelers, but that doesn't mean we skimp on good times. If you enjoy seeing new places, meeting new cats around the country, get a certain thrill from successfully bidding and making a no-trump grand slam, and don't mind long stopovers, look no further.

WHAT'S IN OUR BEDROOM: Complimentary wet-naps, motel soaps and shower caps, ketchup "snack" packets, Styrofoam peanuts, cheat sheet of hobo markings and their meanings, and the world's biggest collection of matchbooks.

WE'RE MOST NEUROTIC ABOUT: Being shipped via air (unpressurized compartments are a hazard of the lifestyle); surly delivery men who ignore the "This End Up" markings on our boxes.

OUR MOTTO: See the world! And let Brown do the driving....

SEX
KITTENS
204

THE LOVE THAT DARE NOT BARK ITS NAME

WHAT I'M LOOKING FOR: CWT iso small-breed male dogs, short-haired only, for hot interspecies commingling. Be house-trained, not too excitable, eager to please but not obsequious. Be able to control your drooling instincts. No terriers and no beagles—a beagle once broke my heart (that's him in the photo).

WHY YOU WANT TO GET TO KNOW ME: I'm a tom with a taste for dog, what can I say? I like your wet rubbery nose, your big ugly paws, your stinky hind leg pits, even your smelly anal glands. My friends can say what they want about me, but I can't help myself. If we really love each other, we can make this crazy thing work.

MY IDEAL DATE INCLUDES: We'll find a nice private place away from prying eyes. I'll clean your coat with my rough, quick tongue; you'll work me over like your favorite chew toy. I'll bite your neck like you're one of the neighborhood toms, you'll try to bury me in the backyard of love.

I'M MOST NEUROTIC ABOUT: My family finding out about my unorthodox tastes.

MY MOTTO: Let's do it doggy style!

SEX KITTENS 205

Accident Victim Seeks Ambulance Chaser

WHAT I'M LOOKING FOR: PAT wants a smart, ambitious prosecuting attorney, P/CA/WT/Q, with a knack for closing cases quickly and the bare minimum of ethics. Single and ready to cross state lines a plus—who knows, if this scam works, we can take the show on the road....

WHY YOU WANT TO GET TO KNOW ME: I'm a perfectly healthy PAT with the acting bug, even if I never perform on the traditional stage. With my purebred good looks, I'm a perfect victim, and I can turn the waterworks on in a heartbeat. With your "legal" skills and my neck cowl, we could make a mint.

WHAT'S IN MY BEDROOM: My prized collection of splints, eye-patches, and crutches. Also, the key to a locker at the bus station, where I keep my "go bag," just in case.

MY IDEAL DATE INCLUDES: I slip on an icy sidewalk in front of a fancy pet-food store. We sue. Using inflammatory, hyperbolic oratory, you bob and weave through your summary before the jury. After a brief recess, the defending attorney gets in touch with a deal to settle. We accept, and it's off to Puerto Rico for a well-earned vacation.

A SECRET MOST OTHERS DON'T KNOW ABOUT ME: I've never been sick in my entire life.

MY MOTTO: It only hurts when I laugh, Your Honor.

SEX KITTENS 206

Victor/Victoria

WHAT I'M LOOKING FOR: CAQ, formerly CAT, iso CAT who can be a loving and tender nurse, possibly more. Must be gentle, kind, able to give love freely. Prefer straight-identifying toms for romance, but I can be flexible depending on the situation. (But not until the stitches come out.)

WHY YOU WANT TO GET TO KNOW ME: I'm a post-op transgender who's ready to start life all over again, this time in the right body. I'm full of passion. I want to get the most I can out of life, and maybe someday settle down with a tom who loves me for me and wants to start a family. Could you be that special one?

I'M MOST NEUROTIC ABOUT: I'm just sorry I didn't take care of this sooner—I've always known I was a queen on the inside, ever since I was a kitten.

BEST/WORST/BIGGEST LIE I EVER TOLD: I still haven't told my family—my father's a career Army cat and I'm afraid he'd never understand.

MY MOTTO: The heart wants what it wants.

SEX KITTENS 207

Let Me Watch

WHAT I'M LOOKING FOR: Sane, normal CAT wants to contact shameless CA/W queen who will let me watch her have a bowel movement. Prefer longhaired queens with fluffy tails. Prefer outdoors over kitty litter, but can accommodate. Must be discreet and hemorrhoid-free.

WHY YOU WANT TO GET TO KNOW ME: I'm a respected family guy in my neighborhood. Well-liked, no fleas, not looking for sex or romance. Just want to see you take care of business, then you can be on your way. Don't worry about covering—I'll do that for you.

WHAT I'M LISTENING TO/WATCHING: On TV: I like the original *CSI*, reruns of *Star Trek: The Next Generation*, and *Law & Order: SVU*. I'm a huge fan of Wagner's *Ring Cycle*.

A SECRET MOST OTHERS DON'T KNOW ABOUT ME: I myself can't even pee in the presence of other cats, or even humans.

MY MOTTO: Can you believe this crap?

Meow!

Thirsty Count Seeks Virgin

What I'm Looking For: Eastern European CWT with mysterious, powerful allure iso virginal PA/W queens for dating, possibly more. You: fair-furred, innocent, and trusting. No blood-borne diseases, please.

Why You Want To Get To Know Me: Although I tend to sleep all day, I really come to life at night. I'm incredibly charming, some might say irresistible, and I have some interesting abilities. For instance, I can make rats, bats, and other rodents come when I call them. With me, you will be able to kiss all that tiresome stalking and hunting bye-bye!

My Ideal Date Includes: You show up at my Gothic manor dressed in a nightgown. Suddenly, you hear a noise and turn to see my brilliant, haunting eyes gazing upon you in the foggy moonlight! Paralyzed by a mixture of arousal and terror, you quiver as I open my mouth to kiss your neck. You are transported to a world of ecstasy somewhere between life and death. If my human's kids have a sleepover, of course, we'll have to do this at your place or we'll never get any privacy.

I'm Most Neurotic About: My human's inexplicable taste for garlic knots.

My Motto: Come to me, children of the night!

SEX KITTENS 209

Bang, Bang, Bang!

From: felines690
Sent: Friday, July 22, 2005 @ 2:30 PM
To: Q/TQ
Subject: RE: Bang, Bang, Bang!

WHAT WE'RE LOOKING FOR: Two CA toms and one CAQ, all 4-5 years old, looking for singles and couples interested in group sex. You: single Q or TQ couple, same age, height/weight unimportant, eager to participate in no-holds-barred erotic encounters. Don't respond if you just like to stand back and watch; we need team players. Some catnip okay but nothing harder.

WHY YOU WANT TO GET TO KNOW US: We're all pretty average house-cats from good homes, but we happen to like group sex. Okay, one of us is a little freaky, but you'll learn to deal with his issues. We're not pushy and won't try to get you to do anything you don't want to do. Plus, if you want, you can be Lucky Pierre!

OUR IDEAL DATE INCLUDES: Lots of room, lots of cats, and lots of love (and a cleaning service).

A SECRET MOST OTHERS DON'T KNOW ABOUT US: One of us has a new family. Another one of us is a former preacher's cat. The freaky one, surprisingly, has no unusual family background.

OUR MOTTO: It takes four (or five, or six) to tango—at least the way we do it.

SEX KITTENS 210

PERSONAL

HARDCORE

WHAT WE'RE LOOKING FOR: Three CWTs iso a beefy, mean CA/WT to play prison guard. You: be aggressive, total top, ready to use your nightstick any way necessary to break us down.

WHY YOU WANT TO GET TO KNOW US: We're bad, bad kitties! We've done terrible things, and don't deserve freedom. If you turn your back on any one of us, even for a second, we might cut you.

WHAT'S IN OUR BEDROOM: Cafeteria-style water and food dishes. A public litter box that faces into the room. Homemade shivs. Our custom-built "prison" cage.

WHAT WE'RE WATCHING: All five seasons of *Oz*. Together, we've probably got all of the episodes memorized, word for word. (Our nicknames are "Keller," "Beecher," and "Sister Pete.")

OUR MOTTO: Like Keller says, "Prison don't make you a bitch; you're born one."

SEX KITTENS 211

Tat Cat Into Inking

WHAT I'M LOOKING FOR: Tattoo artist (CAT), iso P/CAQ to be my lover, my muse, and my blank slate. I want to create my next masterpiece on you. Must be young, aggressive queen with short, light hair. Queens with multiple piercings strongly preferred.

WHY YOU WANT TO GET TO KNOW ME: I'm a talented, good-looking "modern primitive" really into the alt lifestyle. I believe that inking yourself is one of the ways to get in touch with our primal selves, like back before cats allowed themselves to be domesticated. I've discovered that if done properly, applying a tattoo can be an incredibly erotic experience, both for the artist and the recipient.

WHAT'S IN MY BEDROOM: Several books of tattoo flash, a sketchbook with some intricate patterns I'm working on for a friend, back issues of *Skin Deep* and *International Tattoo Art* magazines.

A SECRET MOST OTHERS DON'T KNOW ABOUT ME: I have a Prince Albert, although since I don't wear pants, I guess it's not that big a secret.

MY MOTTO:
God left us unfinished so we could customize ourselves.

Hottie!

SEX
KITTENS
212

Sink Me, Baby!

From: tom23
Sent: Thursday, August 4, 2005 @ 2:30 AM
To: CWQ
Subject: RE: Sink Me, Baby!

WHAT I'M LOOKING FOR:
CWT iso a fine, confident, sexy CWQ who enjoys the feel of smooth, cool porcelain against her coat. You must be eager to watch as I lap up the sweet, exotic—and strangely erotic—liquid that trickles from the mysterious silver teat.

WHY YOU WANT TO GET TO KNOW ME: Sane and healthy tom with average to above-average looks, smart, funny, a good listener. I'm willing to escort porcelain-curious queens into a new world of sensual pleasures. No Formica freaks, please.

MY IDEAL DATE INCLUDES: A romantic dinner for two followed by a brisk trot around the yard. Once we've worked up a nice sweat we head for the bathroom, where sweet relief in the form of a damp sink basin and a trickle of ambrosia awaits us.

MY MOTTO: Bow before the porcelain god.

SEX
KITTENS
213

I'm Still Dirty

WHAT I'M LOOKING FOR: CWQ iso brave CWT who isn't afraid of a little water. I love baths, especially warm ones with lots of bubbles. ~~Want to meet a tom~~ who'll join me in these aquatic reveries, ~~bathe me, scrub me~~ with a loofah, treat me like the dirty kitty that I am. No sex unless you get me squeaky clean first.

WHY YOU WANT TO GET TO KNOW ME: I'm a high-spirited and creative lover who'll make you work for your reward. I hate wimpy toms, so be aggressive and dominant. I'll fight you the whole way; that had better be how you like it.

WHAT'S IN MY BEDROOM: Travel-size shampoo bottles I pilfered from my person's luggage. An old rubber ducky, a worn washcloth I sleep on at night.

MY IDEAL DATE INCLUDES: While I roll back and forth outside in the dirt, you'll draw me a nice, hot bath. I'll come in, make eye contact with you, and run like the dickens. You'll chase me all over the house until I'm cornered, then drag me hissing and spitting by the neck to the tub and throw me in. Once I'm shivering and drenched, you climb in on top of me, and together we'll turn this bathtub into a big bowl of love soup.

MY MOTTO: You missed a spot.

Lean On Me

What I'm Looking For: CWT who's into frottage and static looking to rub up against a tight, supple CAQ, any age/race, all night. You: be ample-sized, have healthy, luxurious fur (the longer the better), enjoy the feel of a strong tom rubbing his scent all over your body.

Why You Want To Get To Know Me: I'm funny, down-to-earth, and I treat queens like royalty. If you're with me, you'll get anything you want, day or night, from precision tonguing to extra food. All I ask in return is that you let me caress that smooth frame of yours until I'm ready to explode, or at least until balloons can stick to my fur.

My Favorite Physical Activities: Aside from the above-mentioned fur-on-fur contact, I love to climb under an afghan and roll back and forth, sending little shocks through the afghan and through my own skin. I'd love to double up with a willing queen and see what kind of energy we can generate.

I'm Most Neurotic About: Getting mange.

My Motto: Together we'll make sparks fly. No, seriously.

SEX KITTENS 215

From: queen885
Sent: Tuesday, August 2, 2005 @ 10:26 AM
To: C/PA/WQ
Subject: RE: Wanna Sleepover?

WHAT I'M LOOKING FOR: I'm a CWQ (age 3) who wants to have the biggest slumber party of the year! I'm looking for some fun girls, not for romance (eeew), but friendship. Please be good at gossiping, eating junk food, and playing Truth or Dare. No practical jokers.

WHY YOU WANT TO GET TO KNOW ME: As you can see, I have a large bed space and my humans are hardly ever around. I have unlimited access to food, movies, and make-up (I love to give makeovers!). I'm goofy and funky, and I'd love to share the juicy details of all my secret crushes with some fun 'tweens like myself.

WHAT I'M LISTENING TO/WATCHING: I am obsessed with Christina Aguilera, Jessica Simpson, and Ryan Cabrerra (I am sooo over Britney). My favorite movie is *Mean Girls* and I never miss an episode of *Laguna Beach* or *The O.C.*

A SECRET MOST OTHERS DON'T KNOW ABOUT ME: I had to go to summer school this year.

MY MOTTO: Never be the first one to fall asleep at a slumber party.

Purr-fect!

SEX
KITTENS
216

I'm Miss Fabulous, You Can Be Runner Up

What I'm Looking For: CWT seeks CA/WT to follow in my footsteps, be my assistant, bodyguard, support group of one, publicist, and all-purpose consultant.

Why You Want To Get To Know Me: Because you can't just be fabulous all on your own—it has to be bestowed on you by a member of the aristocracy, like myself. You'll want to get to know me because cats who know me get seen, and then great things follow.

What I'm Watching: *American Idol, Star Search* (both old and new versions), *Fame* (the movie, the series, and the reality show).

My Ideal Date Includes: I love modern dance especially anything by Isadora Duncan (although she turned me off long scarves forever) and, lately, Matthew Bourne. You might think that means I'd like to see a dance performance, but what I'd rather do is find a good open space and explore my natural grace and energy alongside you!

Mo Motto: Don't dream it, be it!

SEX KITTENS 217

Index of Cat Owners

SEX KITTENS 219

Photography Credits

SEX KITTENS 221

65: Sleman, Owe/Stock.XCHNG (Piggy)
66: Hammoudeh, Alaaeddin/Stock.XCHNG
67: Vervaeke, Adam/Stock.XCHNG
68: Walters, Chris (Pazuzu)
69: Woodhull, Victoria (Peaches)
70: Ewing, Brianne (Grizzly, Tully)
71: Nelson, Madeline (Frankie)
72: Turnpaugh, Lisa (Annabelle Noel)
73: Gabriel, Roben (Shadow)
74: Uebbing, Bill (Juliet)
75: Lee, Donna (Mitzi)
76: Hipple, Gloria (Rhett, Silverbridge, Chaucer)
77: Ellis, Jeremy (Disco)
78: Kapala, Ula/Stock.XCHNG
80: Bosley, Sharon (Natasha)
81: Clemons, Katrina "Kat" (Artemis)
82: Threlfall, Rodger/Stock.XCHNG (Little Mo)
83: Zuydweg, Victor/Stock.XCHNG (Singa)
84: Borse, Laura/Stock.XCHNG
85: Hepworth, Connie (Pixie)
86: Koh, Sumi (Sprite)
87: Scholtz, Retha/Stock.XCHNG (Vande Bald's Dante)
88: Kapala, Ula/Stock.XCHNG
89: Kriewaldt, Leslie (Eddie)
90: Endow, Susie (Lily)
91: de Almeida, Michael and Lori (Shelby)
92: Wetherby, Carrie (Tristan)

93: Nouveau, Cristy Gibbs (Peanut)
94: Ramandt, Angelica "Angel" (Johnny Bend)
95: Bocast, Marlene (Ranger)
96: Krause, Brendan and Sue (Barney)
97: Bradley, Pat (Tabby)
98: Garner, Nancy (Oliver)
99: Ruszkai, Jami (Nigel Ruszkai)
100: O'Donnell, Olga and Frank (Sasha)
101: Groff, Melissa (Misty)
102: Garrison, June (Spatz)
103: Bechtloff, Karen and Russ (Mr. Jinx)
104: Fasnacht, Angela (Piper)
105: Bocast, Marlene (Ranger)
106: Schilo, Kristen (Yowza Gato Schilo)
107: Turnpaugh, Lisa (Bella Nina)
108: Turnpaugh, Lisa (Ginger Lily Rose)
109: Rotshenker, Lior/Stock.XCHNG (Tazz)
110: Candice/Stock.XCHNG (Gracie)
111: Gabriel, Roben (Shadow)
112: Bocast, Marlene (Clarence)
113: Uebbing, Bill (Juliet)
114: Lee, Donna (Mitzi)
115: Turnpaugh, Lisa (Annabelle Noel)
116: Palaz, Tulay (tulayp@gmail.com)/ Stock.XCHNG (Zilly)
117: Curley, Nicole and Will (Blue)
118: Hardwick, Bill/Stock.XCHNG (Arthur)
119: Villi, Iva/Stock.XCHNG

120: McCallister, Sara/Stock.XCHNG
121: van den Hurk, Frank/Stock.XCHNG
122: Bauzys, Susan/Stock.XCHNG (Noelle)
123: Tsevis, Charis/Stock.XCHNG
124: Rosen, Shoshana/Stock.XCHNG (Karlos)
125: Swanson, Heather (Lexington)
126: Bocast, Marlene (Mamoru)
127: Klug, Peg (Rocky)
128: Margetts, Michelle (Princess)
129: Humphrey, Rachel (Theo Huxtable)
130: Morrison, Valerie (Gazoo)
131: Schlesak, Lillian (Coco-Nut)
132: Klug, Peg (Rocky)
133: Rieper, Anika (Josephine)
134: Ackerman, Janice (Trudy)
135: Allen, Claudia (Timmy)
136: Collins, Courtney (Bean)
137: Schultz, Ronnie (Jennie)
138: Baysinger, Jennifer (Zack)
139: Klug, Peg (Rocky)
140: Versluis, Robert-Jan/Stock.XCHNG (Plint)
142: Ellis, Jeremy (Disco)
143: Schultz, Ronnie (Kitty)
144: Baysinger, Jennifer (Zack)
145: Foster, Gigi (Pippin)
146: Krause, Brendan and Sue (Boo Boo)
147: Irwin, Kathleen "Kitty" (Coco)
148: Stewart, Allan and Lori Kata

(Abby, also known as Queen Abigail Hermione Anastasia)
149: Ramandt, Angelica "Angel" (Puntje)
150: Rieper, Anika (Josephine)
151: Murry, Brando/Stock.XCHNG
152: Ralphs, Wendy (Wickett)
153: Gatti, Michele/Stock.XCHNG (Raffy)
154: Salisbury, Kam/Stock.XCHNG (Shnooks)
155: Wray, M. Douglas/Stock.XCHNG (Franny)
156: Bocast, Marlene (Ranger)
157: Jones, Marcella (Romeow)
158: Jones, Cory (Bob)
159: Cotton, Robert (Shadow)
160: Rose, Mary (Patches)
161: Patataj/Stock.XCHNG
162: Scholtz, Retha/Stock.XCHNG (Amitola)
163: Zolkiffli, Zaid/Stock.XCHNG
164: Turnpaugh, Lisa (Benjamin Nicholas Bailey)
165: Versluis, Robert-Jan/Stock.XCHNG (Plint)
166: Tamnakpho, Jakrit/Stock.XCHNG
168: Morrison, Valerie (Gazoo)
169: Irwin, Christina (Gypsy)
170: Reiter, Ceasonne (Butters)
171: Groff, Melissa (Misty)
172: Nanasay, Lena (Oliver)

SEX KITTENS
223

173: Paster, Margo (Conchita)
174: Bahneman, Laura (Little Bit)
175: Bocast, Marlene (Ranger)
176: Morris, Shanna (Nails)
177: Turnpaugh, Lisa (Annabelle Noel)
178: Saiya, Abigail (Shelby)
179: Dias, Barbara (Molly)
180: Larson, Mary (Silverado)
181: Pepe, Kathy (Church)
182: Margetts, Michelle (Princess)
183: Rodgers, Jean (Storm Runner)
184: Foster, Gigi (Pippin)
185: Collins, Courtney (Bean)
186: Tamnakpho, Jakrit/Stock.XCHNG
187: Bar, Barbara/Stock.XCHNG (Gabi)
188: Rusin, Krystian/Stock.XCHNG
189: Grist, Anna/Stock.XCHNG (Splat)
190: Glowinski, Nancy (Boris)
191: Swanson, Heather (Lexington)
192: Uzel, Olan/Stock.XCHNG
194: Bosley, Sharon (Xena)
195: Siegel, Joyce (Jones)
196: Allen, Claudia (Benny, Oliver)
197: Martin, Catherine (Patsy, Pez)
198: Gravenese, Carol (Calvin)

199: Pluto, Darline (Munchkin)
200: Nelson, Madeline (Max, Frankie)
201: Ewing, Brianne (Grizzly, Tully)
202: Wetherby, Carrie (Tristan)
203: de Almeida, Lori and Michael
     (Shelby, Max)
204: Bocast, Marlene (Misha,
     Sasha, Kyle)
205: de Boer, Jeroen/Stock.XCHNG
206: Delcado, Mirko/Stock.XCHNG
     (Astrogatto)
207: Trauzzola, Luca/Stock.XCHNG
     (Picchio)
208: Fogh, Louise/Stock.XCHNG
     (Rosa)
209: Unknown
210: Uzel, Olan/Stock.XCHNG
211: Borsh, Julie M./Stock.XCHNG
212: Bocast, Marlene (Clarence)
213: Schlesak, Lillian (Coco-Nut)
214: Lee, Donna (Mitzi)
215: Winder, Celia (Orchid)
216: Woodhull, Victoria (Wolfie)
217: Rodgers, Jean (Gypsy Princess)